# MARITAL THERAPY

# Pergamon Titles of Related Interest

**Kanfer/Goldstein**  HELPING PEOPLE CHANGE, Third Edition
**Masson/O'Byrne**  APPLYING FAMILY THERAPY:
A Practical Guide for Social Workers

# Related Journal

Free sample copies available upon request

CLINICAL PSYCHOLOGY REVIEW

# PSYCHOLOGY PRACTITIONER GUIDEBOOKS

### EDITORS
**Arnold P. Goldstein,** Syracuse University
**Leonard Krasner,** SUNY at Stony Brook
**Sol L. Garfield,** Washington University

# MARITAL THERAPY
## *A Behavioral-*
## *Communications Approach*

## PHILIP H. BORNSTEIN AND
## MARCY T. BORNSTEIN
University of Montana

## PERGAMON PRESS
New York     Oxford     Toronto     Sydney     Frankfurt

Pergamon Press Offices:

**U.S.A.**            Pergamon Press Inc., Maxwell House, Fairview Park,
                     Elmsford, New York 10523, U.S.A.

**U.K.**             Pergamon Press Ltd., Headington Hill Hall,
                     Oxford OX3 0BW, England

**CANADA**           Pergamon Press Canada Ltd., Suite 104, 150 Consumers Road,
                     Willowdale, Ontario M2J 1P9, Canada

**AUSTRALIA**        Pergamon Press (Aust.) Pty. Ltd., P.O. Box 544,
                     Potts Point, NSW 2011, Australia

**FEDERAL REPUBLIC**  Pergamon Press GmbH, Hammerweg 6,
**OF GERMANY**       D-6242 Kronberg-Taunus, Federal Republic of Germany

**BRAZIL**           Pergamon Editora Ltda., Rua Eça de Queiros, 346,
                     CEP 04011, São Paulo, Brazil

**JAPAN**            Pergamon Press Ltd., 8th Floor, Matsuoka Central Building,
                     1-7-1 Nishishinjuku, Shinjuku, Tokyo 160, Japan

**PEOPLE'S REPUBLIC**  Pergamon Press, Qianmen Hotel, Beijing,
**OF CHINA**         People's Republic of China

**Copyright © 1986 Pergamon Press Inc.**

Second printing, 1989

**Library of Congress Cataloging in Publication Data**

Bornstein, Philip H.
    Marital therapy.

    (Psychology practitioner guidebooks)
    Bibliography: p.
    Includes indexes.
    1. Marital psychotherapy. 2. Behavior therapy.
3. Interpersonal communications. I. Bornstein,
Marcy T. II. Title. III. Series. [DNLM:
1. Behavior Therapy. 2. Communication.
3. Marital Therapy. WM 55 B736m]
RC488.5.B648   1985      616.89'156      85-12255
ISBN 0-08-031615-8
ISBN 0-08-031614-X (pbk.)

*Printed in the United States of America*

# Contents

# List of Figures

# List of Tables

# Preface

The evidence is overwhelmingly clear that in today's contemporary society, couples continue to experience intense and pervasive difficulties in the establishment and maintenance of loving, intimate relations. In fact, the problem of marital distress accounts for more mental health referrals than any other psychiatric diagnostic category. Unfortunately, although numerous marital therapy texts exist, none are written explicitly for the professional therapist or counselor. *Marital Therapy: A Behavioral-Communications Approach*, however, is an attempt to remedy this problem. As a consequence, readers will find a comprehensive yet pragmatic model describing applied clinical work with couples. This book should serve as a working tool for students and those employed within the disciplines of clinical/community/school psychology, psychiatry, guidance and counseling, pastoral counseling, social work, and nursing.

The behavioral-communications approach is a theoretical and practical blend of systems, cognitive, and behavioral orientations. This is apparent throughout the book. Although behavior is conceptualized as serving a literal and/or representational purpose, interactions that occur between spouses always have relational outcomes; that is, one partner's behavior has effects upon the other. This clearly is a systemic notion. However, it is recognized that individual attributions and interpretations of partner's behaviors vary widely, affecting spousal perception and the type of response emitted. Indeed, behavior within relationships can be significantly influenced by cognitive factors. Finally, to modify dysfunctional couples' interactions, practitioners may choose to utilize applied principles of objectification, social exchange, reciprocity, problem-solving training, and so on. The technical application of these principles is most certainly behavioral in nature. Thus, the behavioral-communications model presents the reader with a conceptual and clinical treatment package distinguished by an integration of the three most widely accepted theoretical systems of the past decade. However, this book is clearly a practitioner's guide and, as a result, we have purposefully chosen to limit our discussion of theoretical issues. Marital concepts and behavioral-communications principles are presented in the first and second chapters, but from that point onward we have attempted to remain wholly applied in orientation.

There are two major aspects of this application that we would like to note. First, behavioral-communications marital therapy is an orderly yet flexible approach to evaluation and treatment. Following a comprehensive yet practical assessment, therapists implement the principles of behavior change through a variety of tactics, strategies, and procedures. The purpose of these techniques is to clearly set the forces of positive reciprocity in motion. Once this budding foundation of trust has been formed, partners are then taught communications and problem-solving skills, with maintenance of behavior change programmed directly into the treatment model. Thus, behavioral-communications marital therapy actually becomes a five-step procedure:

1. assessment (Chapter 3),
2. tactics of treatment (Chapter 4),
3. communications (Chapter 5),
4. problem-solving (Chapter 6),
5. maintenance (Chapter 7).

As we have already indicated, the steps are not fixed and immutable, but they do appear to be somewhat sequential and organized; that is, one step builds logically upon the other. Certainly, however, the personalistic approach of the therapist and the idiosyncratic needs of the couple will dictate the exact shape and form of each therapeutic endeavor.

The second aspect of application worthy of mention deals with the format of this book. Specifically, the reader will find a variety of case material and therapeutic examples provided throughout the book. Although every effort has been taken to protect the identity of individual clients, we have drawn heavily from our own clinical practice. Thus, the reader is provided with examples from each of the following categories: (a) therapist–client dialogue, (b) edited transcripts, (c) process notes, (d) case records, and (e) therapist recollections. Further, Chapter 8 provides three extended case examples as a demonstration of clinical application from referral through follow-up.

# Acknowledgments

There are a number of people to whom we are truly indebted. First and foremost, we would like to thank our children for their continuing support and unique contributions to this book: To Jordie, for being the marvelous young woman that she is (and doing the laundry); to Hallie, for her effervescent smile (and alphabetizing the references); and to Brette, for the joy that she brings and the person she has become.

Second, a special word of thanks must be extended to our colleagues and graduate student friends in the Department of Psychology at the University of Montana. It is not easy relating to a couple, one part of which is faculty member, the other part graduate student. They did it with ease and made it a pleasure. Third, a note of appreciation to Greg Wilson for his senior contribution to Chapter 3; he is an efficient and amazingly productive young scientist-practitioner. Fourth, with a secretary like Linda Richtmyer, we as authors must never agonize over spelling, punctuation, split infinitives, and so on—she is a word processor, letter-quality printer, and remarkable human being all rolled into one. Fifth, this book would have never happened without the aid of Jerry Frank. From bed and board in Missoula, Montana, to page proofs in Elmsford, New York, Jerry did it all—we are forever grateful. Lastly, we would like to thank each other for the wondrous collaboration of the past 18 years. It has been a sheer delight.

Philip and Marcy Bornstein
April, 1985

# Chapter 1

# Marriage and Marital Therapy: Practical and Conceptual Foundations

## "AND THEY LIVED HAPPILY EVER AFTER?"

Given present trends, one can expect that approximately two and one-half million marriage licenses will be issued in the United States during this year alone (National Center for Health Statistics, 1984). Unfortunately, one can similarly predict that one and one-quarter million divorces will also take place during the same period of time. As crude statistics, these numbers are of no great surprise. However, one must remember that marriage remains the primary emotional and legal commitment we make in our adult life. Moreover, selecting a partner and entering into a marital contract is considered both a maturational milestone and a personal achievement. There is no doubt that the choice of a marital partner is one of the most important decisions we make in our lifetimes. At stake is our future—the challenges, excitement, rearing of children, family planning, income, and responsibility. What then becomes surprising is that 50% of all marriages end in divorce. With this rather astonishing finding as our point of departure, let us begin by examining the process of contemporary mate selection.

## Will You Marry Me?

Available evidence indicates that over 90% of the U.S. population will marry at least once in their lifetimes (Glick, 1984), but it is interesting to note that the basic reasons for contemporary marriage have recently undergone considerable change. Although marriage continues to be part of the fabric of society, parents and matchmakers no longer dictate mate selection. Instead, free choice reigns supreme, or at least it appears to do so (Hatfield & Walster, 1978).

Although marriage remains the universal institution, its purpose ap-

1

pears to have been modified over time. Traditionally, marriage was a means by which society regulated sexual behavior, provided for the bearing of children, and allowed for the economic maintenance of the family unit. How times have changed! Certainly, it is common for young people to become sexually involved today without entering into a marriage agreement. Further, many of those who choose to marry do so with a child-free alternative in mind. Lastly, as the family farm becomes more a part of corporate America and an increasing number of women enter the work force, the economic justification for marriage and family life continues to decrease.

For what fundamental reasons do people marry? We would suggest that there are three primary reasons for marriage in today's society: (a) for love, (b) for companionship, and (c) for expectation fulfillment. "Because we're in love" is the most frequently given explanation for marriage (Knox, 1985). Obviously, the word *love* holds considerably different meaning for different people. In general, however, love refers to a set of deeply held positive feelings directed toward another person. Among these feelings are attachment, caring, intimacy, arousal, passion, rapport, and *suffering* (we will discuss this further in a subsequent section). People also marry, however, for companionship purposes. As defined by Hatfield and Walster (1978), "companionate love is the affection we feel for those with whom our lives are deeply intertwined" (p. 9). It is the type of love based upon a sharing of experience, a love in which we know our partner will always be there, a love wherein we know we will always be accepted for what we are. Finally, today's couples marry for expectation fulfillment purposes as well. As noted by Sager (1976), individuals expect to derive certain benefits both from their partners in particular, and the marriage in general. More importantly, in today's technological and egalitarian society, partners bring to the relationship a heightened sense of expectation. They are no longer content with the role of homemaker or provider but want and expect to achieve nothing short of perfection. This perfection is based upon a naive sense of happiness, fulfillment, and an abiding belief in the ridiculous notion that "love conquers all." In sum, today's couples have been sold a bill of goods. They have accepted the notion that marriage brings with it a fulfillment of their every psychological need. They have bought, hook–line–sinker, fantasized notions of historical romanticism. And it is these unrealistic and idealistic expectations in particular that provide the quicksand of marital disenchantment.

## The Romantic Ideal

Love is perhaps the most elusive of all human emotions. Poets, songwriters, philosophers, and scientists have all taken a stab at defining this enigmatic condition, yet none have successfully done so. Clearly, however, the notion of romantic love persists, and we, in turn, seek out that partner who best exemplifies our personal conception of the romantic ideal.

Romantic love is a relatively new phenomenon. Kurland (1953) reviewed the history of romance and found instances of it dating back to early civilizations (e.g., ancient Rome, Greece, etc.), although most historians agree that romantic love came into prominence during the Middle Ages and is closely associated with the rise of courtly love. This love was asexual in nature, but involved acts of courage and virtue enacted on behalf of one's beloved. It should be noted, however, that courtly love had nothing whatsoever to do with marriage; that is, the love object was both idealized and extramarital in origin.

What are the characteristics of this romantic ideal? A number of elements exist, including the following:

1. Love is a wildly emotional state composed of physiological arousal, confusion of feelings, intense absorption, and overwhelming desire.
2. Love occurs at first sight.
3. Love is blind (i.e., we are oblivious to any faults or limitations in our loved one).
4. Love conquers all (i.e., there is no obstacle great enough to thwart true love).
5. There is but one true love (i.e., there is one special person for everyone, *but only one!*).
6. Love is synonymous with passion and sexual union.
7. Love is both ecstasy and agony.

In addition to the previous list, Tennov (1979) cites other characteristics that lovers possess. These include intrusive thoughts, drastic mood swings, fears of rejection, bodily arousal, and an inexplicable (almost magical) biochemical attraction to one another. In sum, the implications of the romantic ideal are quite clear. First, the onset of love is apt to be sudden and perhaps even highly dramatic. Second, individuals have little control over the entire process and are instead swept away in a sea of raging, sometimes conflicted, emotion. Third, intensity of the love virtually demands that its duration be brief. Examining the situation realistically, we must conclude that if romantic ideals form the initial basis of contemporary marriage, then disappointment, disenchantment, and divorce are sure to soon follow.

## Statistics on Divorce

For a great many American couples, the phrase '' 'til death do us part'' must catch in their throats for reasons of hypocrisy alone. Although the most permanent of intentions may be in effect on one's wedding day, the reality of the situation is a very different matter. Quite simply, for approximately 50% of most couples, their marriage will eventually become obsolete! But let us look more closely at that data.

To begin, there are a variety of ways in which we can examine divorce statistics. First, crude divorce rate provides us with information regarding the number of divorces for every 1,000 members of the population. Although this does give a per capita divorce rate, because not everyone in the society marries, the figure may be biased as the population fluctuates. Second, refined divorce rate provides similar information to the crude rate but is based upon the number of divorces per 1,000 married women over the age of 15 years. Third, we can simply examine the number of marriage licenses and divorce decrees granted within a specified period of time. Fourth, we can longitudinally follow a sample of couples over a prolonged period of time to see what percentage end in divorce, desertion, annulment, and so on. As is probably obvious, each of the above methods has its assets and liabilities. As a consequence, we will try to provide a variety of divorce data.

Marriage continues to be a highly valued and near unanimous activity of most adult Americans. Current estimates indicate that 96% to 97% of the adult population will marry at some point in their lifetimes (Carter & Glick, 1976; Glick & Norton, 1973). Thus, it is not surprising that marriage rates have essentially remained constant over the last 15-year period. In fact, crude marriage rates have basically remained stable at approximately 10.0 per 1,000 population for more than a century. Unfortunately, the same is not true of divorce rates. Current data indicates that the present divorce rate is greater than ever before and that the United States has currently the highest divorce rate in the world.

Table 1.1 indicates the number of divorces and crude divorce rates in the United States over the past 20-year period. As should be evident from these numbers alone, there has been marked increase in both frequency and rate of divorce throughout the length of this period. During the 1920s, one out of seven marriages ended in divorce. By 1950, it had jumped to one in five marriages ending in divorce. And, by 1980, one of every two marriages was dissolved due to divorce. To demonstrate the rapidity with which divorce rates have risen, all one needs to do is peruse data from the National Center for Health Statistics. For example, in 1912, the crude divorce rate was 1.0 per 1,000 population. In 1940, it reached 2.0 per 1,000 population. By 1969, it had surpassed 3.0, and by 1972 it had already exceeded 4.0 per 1,000 population. Further, 4 years later in 1976, divorce rates had already exceeded 5.0 per 1,000 population. In just 7 years (1969–1976), the divorce rate increase was comparable to the increase that had occurred for the entire 57 preceding years (1912–1969). Additionally, the refined divorce rate has more than doubled over the past 15-year period

Table 1.1. Number of Divorces and Crude Divorce Rate,
1965–1984

| Year | Number of Divorces | Divorces Per 1,000 Population (Crude Divorce Rate) |
|------|--------------------|---------------------------------------------------|
| 1965 | 479,000 | 2.5 |
| 1970 | 708,000 | 3.5 |
| 1975 | 1,036,000 | 4.9 |
| 1978 | 1,130,000 | 5.1 |
| 1979 | 1,181,000 | 5.3 |
| 1980 | 1,189,000 | 5.2 |
| 1981 | 1,213,000 | 5.3 |
| 1982 | 1,183,000 | 5.1 |
| 1983 | 1,179,000 | 5.0 |
| *1984 | 1,175,000 | 5.0 |

*National Center for Health Statistics estimate (1984).

(1965: 10.6 divorces per 1,000 married women over age 15 years; 1980: 22.6 divorces per 1,000 married women over age 15 years). Finally, the number of years until divorce has progressively decreased in accord with the previous figures. Specifically, of those couples married in 1950, 25% were divorced within 25 years; of those marrying in 1952, 25% were divorced within 20 years; of those marrying in 1959, 25% were divorced within 15 years; by 1965, 25% were divorced within 10 years; and today, approximately 25% are divorced within 3 years of their vows (see Figure 1.1).

In sum, the average divorcing couple will stay married for approximately 7 years. Following divorce, 80% of these individuals will eventually remarry. Between marriages, the trials and tribulations of their new-found singlehood will last for an average of 3 years (Glick, 1980). Unfortunately, available evidence indicates that second marriages are even more likely to terminate in dissolution, with 60% ending in divorce (Glick, 1984). However, of those remarrieds who stay married, they appear to be as successful and happy as do first-marrieds (Glenn & Weaver, 1977; Weingarten, 1980). Of those who eventually divorce, the mean length of second marriages is only 5 years, and the problems experienced may be considerably different from those of first-marrieds. In either case, though, there appears to be a broad variety of factors that influence the above-noted divorce trends.

## Factors Influencing Divorce

The question as to what goes wrong within an individual marriage is not a simple one to answer. In fact, in our judgment there are a myriad of factors that may influence a couple's decision to separate and perhaps even-

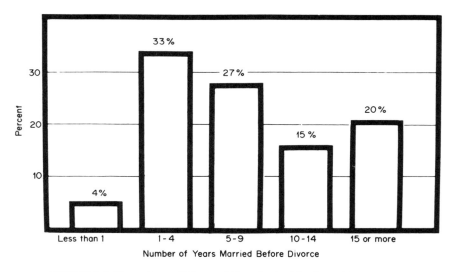

FIGURE 1.1. Percentage of Divorced Couples by Number of Years Married

tually divorce. For didactic purposes, we have classified these factors into three categories: social, personal, and relationship.

*Social Factors.* We are currently living in an era of unprecedented change. Things happen so quickly that even experts in specialized fields of study find that they cannot keep up with developments in their own narrow area of expertise. Moreover, the complexity and impersonalization of society-at-large only goes to further one's sense of alienation, isolation, and pervasive global distrust. It is during such periods of rapid change that our values, beliefs, and customs are constantly called into question and threatened on all fronts. This is no more apparent than in the area of marital and family relations.

The traditional monogamous marriage no longer holds a monopoly on the forms of union that a couple may pursue. Since the 1960s, we have witnessed the rise of alternative life-styles. Among the options now available to individuals are: (a) cohabitation, (b) gay marriage, (c) "swinging," (d) open marriage, (e) group or communal marriage, (f) remarriage, and (g) the sexually active single's life-style. In essence, people may choose to leave a traditional marriage not because it is terribly dissatisfying, but rather because it is less attractive to them than the other options that formerly did not exist.

Even within marriage, however, sex roles and relationships are changing with the growing egalitarianism in society. Marriage is not as easy as it used to be because things are not as well-defined as they used to be. In the traditional marriage, everyone knew their places: husband provided authority and financial support, wife was responsible for housekeeping and childrearing. Today the situation has changed dramatically: Responsibilities now are either shared or determined on a more idiosyncratic basis. The result of this change is quite clear. When one's personal needs and goals go unsatisfied, an individual asks: "Why should I stay in this relationship when I'm giving a lot and getting very little in return?"

Somewhat related to the above, the majority of contemporary marriages now involve dual-worker couples, with a husband and wife both working outside the home in career-oriented positions. The net effect of this development is of overwhelming importance. Partners may be pulled in different directions and forced to pursue substantially different goals. Time together may be limited, preoccupation heightened, and external sources of stress generally increased. Over time, people grow further apart, increasing both their emotional and physical distance from one another.

It was not long ago that divorce was generally considered scandalous. Once again, how times have changed! Not only is divorce no longer "the family disgrace," it is now thoroughly commonplace. Divorce has become a more-than-reasonable solution to a less-than-reasonable situation. Clearly, there are those who question whether the move toward divorce occurs too rapidly, too impulsively, and too revengefully (Crosby, 1985). In any case, the moral, religious, economic, and social sanctions no longer apply. Divorce is readily available and rampant in the environment. As recently noted by a male client engaged in marital therapy, "Sure, we might as well divorce—everybody else is doing it."

Finally, prime social factors having some influence over divorce rate are the legal reforms adopted within the past 15 years, most notably the move toward "no-fault" divorce. In 1970, California abolished the concept of fault in divorce proceedings. In so doing, "irreconcilable differences leading to the immediate breakdown of the marriage" was substituted in its place. This landmark piece of legislation has revolutionized the ease and convenience with which divorce may be obtained. As of 1984, only two states (Illinois and South Dakota) had not adopted some form of no-fault divorce legislation. In sum, the notions of adultery, mental/ physical cruelty, and desertion are on the verge of becoming anachronisms. Although they certainly continue to exist, no-fault legislation has undoubtedly increased the social acceptability of marital dissolution.

*Personal Factors.* Obviously, there is a wealth of personal factors that may contribute to and exacerbate marital dissatisfaction. As indicated earlier in this chapter, we firmly believe that the misperceptions and unrealistic expectations frequently brought into the marriage are prime examples of such personal factors. So long as society continues to foster, and individuals continue to adopt romantic ideals and fantasized expectations, marital disillusionment will thrive. During the course of marital therapy, we have personally witnessed so many of these expectations that the list is virtually endless. However, for purposes of explication, here is a sampling of some of the more common false hopes, which could be called The 12 Deadly Expectations of Marriage.

1. "Our love (i.e., romance and excitement) will continue unabated over time."
2. "My spouse should be able to anticipate my thoughts, feelings, and needs."
3. "My husband/wife would never hurt me or strike back in anger."
4. "If you truly loved me, you would always try to please me (i.e., meet my every need and desire)."
5. "Love means never having to be angry or upset with your partner."
6. "Love means always wanting to be together."
7. "Our personal interests, goals, and values will always remain the same."
8. "My partner will always be open, direct, and honest with me."
9. "Because we are in love, my spouse will always respect, understand, and accept me no matter what I might do."
10. "It would be terrible if my husband/wife ever embarrassed, belittled, or criticized me."
11. "Our level of sex, affection, and commitment must never decline."
12. "We must always be in agreement with one another on matters of import."

As false hopes and unrealistic goals, each of the above only serves to drive couples into further despair, disappointment, frustration, and anger. Thus, one of the goals of therapy is surely to question, clarify, and challenge these unrealistic and self-defeating notions.

Other factors that contribute to the increased divorce rate are the personal values and goals adopted by the individuals within the relationship. In particular, many individuals enter into marital union with the avowed goal of happiness. When that momentarily wanes or when marital satisfaction begins to decline, their solution may lie in dissolution. Indeed, as noted by Prochaska and Prochaska (1978), we live in a self-actualizing era. Consequently, any action taken in the name of becoming one's best and truest self is apt to be applauded, even if it means withdrawing from one's marriage and family.

In a related manner, it must be recognized that people do change. At the point when marriage is first considered, partners' interests and activities may be highly congruent. Within a short period of time, however, spousal interests may develop along highly divergent routes. Thus, as individuals personally change, so changes the relationship. When partners can no longer find overlapping sets of interests, activities, and values, they begin the symbolic process of withdrawal.

Lastly, as undoubtedly is apparent, each partner brings to the marital situation a unique personal and psychological history. For example, one's own family of origin certainly will influence the likelihood of marital separation or divorce (Kaslow, 1981). Simply stated, effective marital role models increase the probability that marital partners will be able to deal with the complexities of their day-to-day living arrangements. Similarly, one's psychological history and current psychological state will either detract from or facilitate marital harmony. Severe psychological distress is apt to wreak havoc both on the individual and the relationship. On the other hand, those individuals who have their own personal "house in order" are most able to set their conjugal one in order as well.

*Relationship Factors.* Up to this point, we have discussed societal and personal factors that influence a couple's decision to live together or apart. Specifically, it would appear that societal factors provide practitioners with a framework for understanding couples' interactions within the larger sociocultural context. Personal factors, on the other hand, allow us to gain a conceptualization and insight into the individual and his/her personal dynamics. However, it is the relationship factors that actually lay the basis for most marital therapy interventions. Quite simply, relationship problems are most effectively treated by relationship therapies (Gurman & Kniskern, 1978). As a consequence, the majority of this book will focus upon therapeutic tactics that may be employed for given relationship problems. What, then, are the most common relationship difficulties?

First, distressed couples tend to exhibit either low rates of pleasing behavior and/or high rates of displeasing behavior (Jacobson & Bussod, 1983). It logically follows that for each spouse, marital satisfaction is therefore a function of the pleasing-to-displeasing ratio (i.e., reward/cost ratio). The more dissatisfying the relationship, the greater the likelihood of divorce. Second, distressed couples typically experience problems in the realm of communications. Specifically, either they repeatedly engage in ineffectual patterns of communication, or problems of intent versus impact are rampant (Gottman, 1979). Once again, we would expect that the more severe these difficulties, the greater the prospects for dissolution. Third, it is not the existence of conflict per se that differentiates distressed from nondistressed relationships. Rather, it is the couple's response to conflict that is of prime importance. The research in this area is very clear—distressed couples exhibit greater difficulty in reaching satisfactory resolution in their problem-solving attempts (Jacobson & Margolin, 1979).

Consequently, divorce is apt to be the direct result of inadequate conflict-resolution skills.

In summary, there is a host of factors that influence decisions about divorce. Couples bring to their marriage both personal needs and socio-cultural influences. However, the problems of the relationship itself may sow the deadliest seeds of all. This may take a variety of forms, including low rates of reward, communications difficulties, and/or negligible conflict-resolution skills. Moreover, these difficulties may center on specific issues (i.e., sex, money, independence, etc.) or pervasively cut across all spheres of interaction. In either case (at least for the present), spouses live together and have effects upon one another. They are interdependent. Thus, to understand individual behavior within a relationship, we must understand the function that behavior serves within the relationship. Yet, we may be placing the conceptual cart before the horse at this point, for there is one final pragmatic issue that deserves our attention before attempting to integrate some of the previously mentioned notions. That is, just what are the effects of marital dissolution in today's society?

## The Effects of Divorce

Divorce has become so commonplace that it is now virtually a part of marriage. Individuals marry, divorce, and remarry at a rate that is surpassed only by the speed with which they buy and sell their automobiles. Serial monogamy has become the order of the day. Unfortunately, many individuals are not prepared for the pain and trauma they will experience as a result of the divorce process. In fact, as indicated by Albrecht (1980), nearly 25% of all individuals view their own divorce as a nightmarish experience. Certainly, this need not always be the case, but our purpose is neither to outline the disastrous nor joyous qualities of divorce. Rather, it is to examine the consequences of divorce as a means of shedding further light on the institution of marriage itself. With that goal in mind, let us briefly explore the positive and negative effects of divorce for both husband and wife. The reader should note that although the "children of divorce" literature may be enlightening, its relevance to the present thesis is quite limited and therefore will not be discussed. Excellent reviews of this research, however, are provided in a variety of sources (Atkeson, Forehand, & Rickard, 1982; Bornstein, 1985; Hetherington, 1979; Kurdek, 1981).

Certainly, not all divorces bring negative consequences. For many, divorce is a godsend. Harmful, destructive, and enormously painful relationships may end and in their place vibrant, exciting, and meaningful relationships may form. The new-found freedom and change of routine may be overwhelmingly positive. Couples may have experienced conflict for years, and divorce can bring the opportunity for a relatively conflict-free existence. In addition, two other aspects of divorce increase the likelihood of personal reward: First, the opportunity to once again be fully in control of one's own life, to no longer have to worry what effect your actions will have upon your spouse's attitude or behavior; second, in those instances where children are involved, knowing that one can act in his/her child's best interests without having to fear constant intrusive opposition from a partner. In essence, life becomes easier because both tension level and the sheer number of conflict-laden incidents are reduced.

The reality of the situation, however, is that most individuals experience great pain as a result of divorce. This pain is most often manifested in the form of disorganization, loneliness, loss of identity, anxiety, a sense of failure, depression, hurt, and/or guilt. It is our feeling that the majority of these negative emotions are the result of three interrelated factors, and moreover, that these factors provide us with information regarding the institution of marriage. They are as follows:

1. Divorce finalizes the fact that intimacy will never be achieved with one's ex-spouse.
2. Divorce creates a ''new you,'' which can be very awkward, uncomfortable, and threatening.
3. Divorce breaks one's daily routine and thereby forces the creation of very practical changes in one's everyday existence.

Collectively, these factors address a number of reasons why people marry. Obviously, most individuals are desirous of forming that intimate, rewarding, loving relationship with another human being. Quite simply, divorce tells them ''it ain't going to happen, at least not right now.'' Further, divorce creates singlehood, displaced homemakerhood, bachelorhood, and so on. These are not roles with which the recently divorced are familiar, nor are they roles that many people easily adopt. Finally, most individuals like some semblance of order, regularity, and consistency in their lives. Without predictability, life would be nothing but chaos. The very practical changes brought forth by divorce (e.g., deciding who makes the lunches, takes the children to school, repairs the garage door, etc.) can be devastating. Given the above, it is truly a wonder that as many as 20% of divorced individuals find the process of dissolution ''relatively painless'' (Albrecht, 1980).

In conclusion, we have attempted to look at marriage in the 1980s from the perspective of the romantic ideal, why people marry, why people divorce, divorce statistics, and the effects of divorce. In so doing, we have generated a variety of notions that form the basis of our conceptualization of marriage and marital relationships. It is to those that we now turn.

# CONCEPTUAL TENETS
# OF MARRIAGE AND MARITAL
# RELATIONSHIPS

Conceptual foundations aid in understanding human behavior. Without such foundations, treatment would appear haphazard, disorganized, and random in nature. Furthermore, the technical tools of therapy are a direct outgrowth of the conceptual model employed. As a consequence, this selection will examine the basic tenets of a behavioral-communications model of marital discord.

## The Couple As System

Psychology as the study of behavior has traditionally been oriented toward the individual. That is, intrapsychic processes are studied, and meaning is derived by understanding the individual as a person. This individualistic philosophy pervades traditional assessment, diagnostic, treatment, and evaluation functions. Although we have no argument with the notion that psychopathology *can* be individually oriented, we see no reason why individual process should have a run on the market. Quite simply, we instead prefer to conceptualize behavior as potentially a function of intraindividual and/or interpersonal factors. Moreover, when problems exist within the marital dyad, clearly such problems are most aptly treated when the relationship rather than the individual is defined as the identified "patient."

Within a behavioral-communications model, spousal behavior is always examined within its relational context. This is not a denial of individual process, but rather an assertion of interactional process as well. In essence, sometimes smoking a cigar is smoking a cigar, but sometimes smoking a cigar is a way to tell your partner "I really don't give a damn about what you like!" Thus, although behavior may be a personalistic statement of an individual's needs, it may also serve a very clear function within the marital dyad. The model, therefore, proposes that spousal behavior may serve both a literal and representational purpose in the relationship.

Given this, it should be obvious that marital therapists will be most interested in observing the transactions that occur between individuals. Behavior does not occur in a vacuum, but rather in relation to other objects, persons, and events. Further, as changes occur within individuals, these changes are apt to have effects throughout the system. Indeed, such effects should be measurable in the behavioral and relational outcomes that are produced. In fact, the relational function of all behavior is best understood by examining the outcome produced (Alexander & Parsons, 1982). That is, the function of Spouse A's behavior is most evident by observing Spouse A, Spouse B, and the resulting effect that is produced between Spouse A and Spouse B. Therefore, it is incumbent upon the effective marital therapist to be extremely well-versed both in intra- and interpersonal change processes.

## Reinforcement/Punishment Rate

A social exchange model of marital interaction clearly assumes that individuals enter and stay in intimate relationships only so long as that relationship is adequately satisfying with respect to both rewards and costs (Thibaut & Kelley, 1959). With this as an initial premise, marital discord is first conceptualized as a function of reinforcement and punishment rates. Reinforcement/reward is perhaps more appropriately termed satisfaction, and punishment/cost more appropriately referred to as dissatisfaction. Thus, exchange theory posits the notion that individuals seek to maximize satisfaction and minimize dissatisfaction.

But, how does one accomplish this? Perhaps with great difficulty, especially when we increase the complexity of our analysis by considering both partners simultaneously, for, in reality, reinforcers and punishers are two entirely different events that may be emitted by two entirely different people. Let us use the hypothetical case of Scott and Andrea:

1. Scott maximizes reward/minimizes cost when Andrea has satisfied his needs and not increased his displeasure.
2. Scott further minimizes his punishment when the behaviors he implements for Andrea are of limited personal cost to him (i.e., create little displeasure for him).
3. Andrea maximizes reward/minimizes cost when Scott has satisfied her needs and not increased her displeasure.
4. Andrea further minimizes her punishment when the behaviors she implements for Scott are of limited personal cost to her (i.e., create little displeasure for her).

The dilemma, of course, lies in the fact that both Scott and Andrea want to maximize satisfaction without increasing their costs. To provide great pleasure to one's partner at a minimum of cost is not easy. Obviously, if the process becomes too painful, the provision of partner rewards is made with great resentment. Therefore, partner-provided satisfactions should be behaviors highly appreciated by the receiver and easily administered by the giver. This makes good common sense and explains why individuals with similar interests will find each other so highly reinforcing—it's easy to please your partner because you find it pleasing yourself.

A final point with respect to reinforcement/punishment rates relates to the fact that there are a variety of ways in which couples may experience distress. Current research appears to indicate that the positive and negative aspects of a relationship are relatively independent of one another (Bornstein, Anton, Harowski, Weltzien, McIntyre, & Hocker, 1981; Bornstein, Hickey, Schulein, Fox, & Scolatti, 1983; Weiss, 1978). Specifically, reducing the displeasurable aspects of the relationship will decrease aversiveness but tend to have a very limited effect on increasing positives. Similarly, improving satisfaction by increasing positives will have only a marginal effect on the reduction of negatives. Thus, it should be apparent that marital distress may result from any of the following factors:

1. low rates of reward,
2. high rates of punishment,
3. low rates of reward and high rates of punishment.

Clearly, however, the experimental evidence overwhelmingly indicates that dysfunctional couples experience lower rates of pleasing and higher rates of displeasing behavior as opposed to normal couples (Bornstein, Bach, Heider, & Ernst, 1981).

## Reciprocity

Jacobson and Margolin (1979) have stated that "there is no concept which is more salient to the behavioral treatment of couples than the principle of reciprocity" (p. 40-41). Quite simply, reciprocity addresses the rate of reinforcement return in ongoing, extended relationships. Moreover, it accomplishes this both on a moment-to-moment and long-term basis.

There are a number of reciprocity factors that warrant our attention. First, within a contemporaneous sequence of events, the norm of reciprocity would predict that you get what you give. That is, distressed couples appear to be more immediately reactive to partner's comments and actions than are nondistressed couples. Second, this immediate reactivity is even more apparent in the area of negative interaction (Gottman, Markman, & Notarius, 1977; Jacobson, Waldron, & Moore, 1980), where distressed individuals are more likely than nondistressed individuals to reciprocate their spouse's use of punishment. Consequently, within a distressed relationship, when one member of the dyad feels "abused," he/she is apt to retaliate with similar "abuse" as soon as possible. Third, research in this area indicates that all couples tend to produce highly correlated rates of rewarding and punishing exchanges on individually selected days (Wills, Weiss, & Patterson, 1974). In other words, there is an equality or parity within positive and negative categories established by husbands and wives on a daily basis. Finally, as noted by Gottman and colleagues (Gottman, Notarius, Markman, Bank, Yoppi, & Rubin, 1976), this parity is most evident over extended periods of time. In fact, their "bank account" model of marital exchange addresses the balanced nature of marital relations from a much wider perspective. Good faith deposits are made, thereby allowing nondistressed couples to move forward in the relationship without immediate positive or negative reciprocation  Distressed couples, on the other hand, have not yet developed the trust that would enable them to function as effectively as those couples with a history of repeated positive deposits.

## Communications Skills

The most frequent problem cited by dissatisfied couples is a failure to communicate. Although this commonsensical notion has been rather widely accepted over the years, it is only recently that researchers have scientifically examined its accuracy. The results of these investigations quite clearly indicate that communications difficulties are not the sole cause of marital conflict. However, communications problems do mark the relationships of distressed couples and appear to exacerbate the difficulties already being experienced.

Weiss and his associates (Birchler, Weiss, & Vincent, 1975; Vincent, Friedman, Nugent, & Messerly, 1979; Vincent, Weiss, & Birchler, 1975) have conducted a series of programmatic investigations observing couples as they attempt to communicate in both conflict resolution and casual conversation tasks. Their findings indicate a higher frequency of negative behaviors among distressed couples on both sets of tasks. Moreover, because these same findings do not occur in conversations with strangers, it would appear that the communications problems are specific to the couple and not the individual.

Gottman and his colleagues have similarly conducted a series of direct observational communications studies (Gottman, 1979). For our present purposes, their findings can be summarized as four major points:

1. When engaged in laboratory conversation, distressed couples exhibit significantly more negative nonverbal behavior than nondistressed couples.

2. Distressed couples have a higher likelihood of engaging in negative reciprocity than nondistressed couples—that is, a negative from Partner A tends to prompt a negative from Partner B.

3. Distressed and nondistressed couples differ in the ways they engage in conflict resolution discussions. Nondistressed couples employ validation loops at the beginning of their discussions, wherein one partner states the problem and the second partner indicates some form of agreement or support. Distressed couples, on the other hand, enter into repetitive, cross-complaining loops. In so doing, they alternatively take turns shar-

ing their complaints without ever attempting to validate their partner's concerns.

4. Distressed and nondistressed couples do not differ in their reported message intent. That is, the messages intended to be sent to their partners were of the same mean value of positiveness. However, the messages received (i.e., impact) by distressed partners were consistently rated as less positive than those received by nondistressed partners. Thus, although distressed couples may be moderately well-intentioned in their remarks, their comments are apt to be more often misperceived than those of nondistressed couples.

Finally, Jacobson et al. (1980) asked distressed and nondistressed couples to complete a lengthy behavioral checklist and global marital satisfaction ratings on a daily basis. Their results indicated that daily satisfaction ratings for distressed couples were best predicted by the general category "negative communication and interaction." Interestingly, daily satisfaction for nondistressed couples was best predicted by "positive communication and interaction." In sum, when taken collectively, these studies clearly indicate that marital dissatisfaction is associated with communications deficits. Specifically, these deficits may be most apparent when couples interact regarding matters of conflict and disagreement. It is to just that topic that we now turn.

## Problem-Solving

Although it should now be obvious that communication skill is a critical variable that differentiates distressed from nondistressed couples, there is yet another aspect to this analysis. Specifically, this communication deficit becomes of overwhelming importance when couples find themselves in conflict. Conflict is a necessary by-product of living together. More importantly, however, couples must find acceptable ways of resolving conflict and dealing with disputes.

Marital and family therapists of various persuasions have generally agreed that ongoing relationships require some semblance of order and regularity (see Gurman & Kniskern, 1981). Family systems simply cannot function smoothly and/or effectively unless a division of responsibilities, rules, and obligations has been put into place. Unfortunately, there are times when either one member of the dyad is desirous of unilaterally changing the rules by which the couple functions, or both members of the dyad cannot reach agreement regarding operational procedures. It is under these circumstances that conflict resolution and problem-solving tactics are required.

Behavior therapists have long recognized the ineffective negative strategies that are sometimes employed in an effort to create change in relationships. Among the most powerful of such strategies is coercion (Patterson & Reid, 1970). In coercive exchanges, one member employs negative reinforcement in return for a positive reinforcer from his/her spouse. This clearly is an aversive control strategy. Consider, for example, the husband who demands that his wife engage in some sexual act that he finds particularly arousing. Each time he approaches her, however, she manages to decline his invitation. Finally out of anger and frustration, he becomes verbally abusive and threatens to begin seeing other women. At this point, she gives in and reluctantly agrees to engage in the desired activity. What has happened here? We would suggest the following:

1. The wife has reinforced her husband's use of a coercive control strategy.
2. In future such encounters, he is apt to once again demand and threaten as a means of achieving his goal.
3. The wife, in turn, has been negatively reinforced for compliance in that her behavior eventually resulted in the cessation of an aversive stimulus (i.e., husband's demands and threats).

Obviously, although both members of the dyad may have received some reinforcement, the means by which this was achieved was far from positive. In fact, the process was highly destructive. Indeed, as noted by Jacobson (1981), the research results in this area generally support the notion that distressed couples tend to produce behavior change through the strategic employment of aversive control tactics (i.e., administration of punishment and withdrawing of rewards). There seems to be no doubt that more positive forms of control could more effectively bring about one's desired goals. Problem-solving, as the process by which couples work toward conflict resolution and explicit agreement, is the means by which this may be achieved.

## Cognitive Factors

To be sure, cognitions are playing a greater and greater role in contemporary approaches to conceptualization and treatment of disordered behavior. Witness the exponential growth in the area of cognitive behavior modification (Bornstein, Kazdin, & McIntyre, 1985). Indeed, a similar kind of revolution also exists in the marital therapy arena, and cognitive factors are assuming greater importance in our understanding of marital dynamics and relationship change (Baucom, 1981; Epstein, 1982; Jacobson, McDonald, Follette, & Berley, in press).

As was discussed earlier in this chapter, individuals bring to the marital union a set of expectations, beliefs, and fantasies regarding both their partner's and their own role in the relationship. Unfortunately, many of these expectations may be highly unrealistic and thereby causal in the development of disappointment, distrust, and hostility. Indeed, Epstein and Eidelson (1981) found that measures of unrealistic relationship beliefs were strong predictors of both marital distress and negative expectations of therapy. As a consequence, they suggest that treatment programs for relationship dysfunction must include some dyadically based cognitive restructuring components. Although they have not as of yet provided a comprehensive listing of the unrealistic relationship beliefs that may affect marital adjustment, their Relationship Beliefs Inventory (Eidelson & Epstein, 1982) is a first step in the marital cognitive assessment area. This inventory examines five such beliefs:

1. disagreement is destructive,
2. mindreading is expected,
3. partners cannot change,
4. sexual perfection,
5. sex-role rigidity (i.e., men and women differ in their relationship needs).

Their results indicated that all of these beliefs were negatively correlated with marital adjustment. Obviously, there are additional unrealistic beliefs that may similarly influence marital functioning (e.g., see The 12 Deadly Expectations of Marriage p. 8). However, empirical verification must await further experimental research.

Of the various cognitive theories that have been proposed in an attempt to explicate marital conflict, attributional models (Kelley, 1973) have received considerable attention. The basic hypothesis is that the causal inferences that spouses derive from observations of their partners' behavior strongly influence their level of satisfaction in the relationship. Specifically, Jacobson et al. (in press) have found that distressed couples attribute their partners' uncooperative and negative behavior to internal factors, thereby insuring their maximal negative impact. Conversely, nondistressed couples were more likely to attribute their partners' rewarding and positive behaviors to internal factors. The end result for both types of couples is maintenance of current satisfaction levels. Distressed couples accentuate their partner's negative behavior and discount the positive; nondistressed couples accentuate the positive and discount the negative acts that may have been committed.

Interestingly, Baucom (1981) has combined some of the above work in the areas of unrealistic expectation and marital attribution and developed a treatment program directed at changing these unproductive and distorted marital cognitions. To accomplish this, he first focused on attributional style with an emphasis on the following dimensions: internal versus external, global versus specific, and stable versus unstable. In later sessions, Ellis's (1962) individual irrational beliefs and Eidelson and Epstein's (1982) unrealistic relationship beliefs are presented and discussed.

Rather than attempting to directly change undesirable partner behavior, Baucom in essence is advocating that the dissatisfied spouse's expectations and beliefs be reexamined and perhaps modified.

A final, although clearly significant, cognitive influence in our conceptual model relates to partners' appraisals of the reward/cost matrix available in alternative relationships. In essence, partners "weigh" the rewards/costs offered by their present partner against the rewards/costs potentially offered by other partners (regardless of whether such partners currently exist in their social network) or nonpartners. As noted by Gurman and Kniskern (1981), this comparison level is probably mediated by a person's own estimation of his/her personal worth and the associated environmental contingencies. Thus, although the reward/cost ratio may favor Partner 1 over Partner 2, other mediational factors may force one to choose the counteralternative. In any case, by cognitively comparing the estimated outcomes of one relationship with another (or no relationship), individuals determine their degree of commitment to continuing in their marriage. This, of course, is a relatively simplified analysis that does not take into account distortions, developmental perspectives, personal history, and so on. However, for our current purposes, the significant point is that cognitive mechanisms certainly impact relationship choices.

## SUMMARY

Available evidence indicates that well over 90% of the U.S. population will marry at least once in their lifetimes. Obviously, people marry for a variety of reasons, among them being: (a) for love, (b) for companionship, and (c) for expectation fulfillment. Regardless of why people marry, however, current statistics indicate that approximately 50% of all marriages end in divorce. The factors that influence divorce can be divided into social, personal, and relationship categories. Although the course may vary for different individuals, the end result tends to be anxiety, pain, depression, hurt, and guilt. A behavioral-communications model of marriage and marital discord takes into account these factors and attempts to utilize them in creating an effective intervention program. The conceptual tenets of this model are as follows:

1. Spousal behavior must always be examined within its relational context.
2. Marital discord is a function of receiving low rates of pleasing behavior and/or high rates of displeasing behavior from one's spouse.
3. Reciprocity occurs in both distressed and nondistressed relationships with negative exchange having an even higher probability of occurrence in distressed relations.

4. Marital dissatisfaction is clearly associated with communications deficits.
5. Dysfunctional couples have great difficulty resolving conflict and effectively dealing with disputes.
6. Cognitive mechanisms certainly influence marital adjustment and satisfaction.

Given these as first principles, the remainder of the book will explicate the behavioral-communications treatment model that follows from the previous list.

# Chapter 2
# Principles of Relationship Change

A behavioral-communications model of effective marital treatment is based on a number of interrelated principles. In this chapter we will first introduce these principles. Throughout the remainder of the book we will then attempt to systematically demonstrate their applied value in actual clinical practice. It should be understood that the material presented herein is an outgrowth of our previously elaborated conceptual tenets and forms the foundation of the behavioral-communications treatment model. Five principles will be discussed: (a) creating a positive working relationship, (b) understanding behavior, (c) objectification, (d) behavioral exchange, and (e) compromise.

## CREATING A POSITIVE WORKING RELATIONSHIP

Perhaps the most essential ingredient of all interpersonal transactions is the establishment of an effective working relationship. In marital therapy, we believe that this involves three major aspects: (a) interpersonal skills of the therapist, (b) tactical skills of the therapist, and (c) building a working relationship between partners.

### Interpersonal Skills of the Therapist

Psychotherapy is a behavior-influence process. Quite frankly, this process has a higher likelihood of success when both parties (i.e., therapist and client) have a mutual respect and appreciation for one another. In fact, there is more than ample research support (Alexander, Barton, Schiavo, & Parsons, 1976; Stuart & Lott, 1972; Weathers & Liberman, 1975) indicating that therapists' interpersonal style critically influences client response to intervention strategies. Let us look then at some of these key interpersonal variables.

*Self-confidence.* There appears to be a direct relationship between one's ability to display self-confidence and the perception of professional competence. Therapists who behave confidently are evaluated by clients as generally more skilled and more effective (Frank, 1961; Goldstein, 1962). Thus, therapists must exhibit those behaviors that increase clients' expectations that they are working with highly professional, skilled, and self-assured individuals. The details of how this can be accomplished will be presented in Chapter 4 (Therapeutic Tactics, Strategies, and Procedures). However, content areas where it is most appropriate to demonstrate self-confidence include: allaying client anxiety, providing a conceptualization of problems, outlining the course of treatment, giving statements regarding likelihood of improvement, and providing continuous feedback regarding progress or lack thereof. Of course, therapist self-confidence should be somewhat reality-based rather than a fraudulent attempt to deceive and manipulate. The latter is both unwarranted and unethical.

*"Human-ness."* People enter into marital therapy with some rational and some irrational ideas about their therapists. Perhaps the most significant of these is that a therapist will be understanding, nonblaming, fair, and relatively "normal." Not long ago, one of us (PHB) had the following interchange take place at the close of an initial therapy session:

> *Client:* You know, you're not at all what I expected.
> *Therapist:* Is that right? Just what did you expect?
> *Client:* Oh, I don't know. Somebody older, I guess.
> *Therapist:* Uh huh.
> *Client:* Yeah, older and with a beard. (*embarrassed laugh*)
> *Therapist:* Sounds like you expected this Dr. Bornstein guy to be a little strange. (*smiling*)
> *Client:* Well, to tell you the truth, I didn't know what to expect but . . . it didn't turn out to be that bad.
> *Therapist:* You mean I didn't live up to your worst expectations? (*smiling*)
> *Client:* No, I guess not. In fact, you really do seem okay.
> *Therapist:* Well, you don't know me very well yet. Once you get to know me then you'll see just how weird I really am! (*laughing*)

The previous exchange clearly exemplifies those interpersonal "humanness" skills to which we are referring. To build a positive working relationship, clients need to know that their therapists are reasonable, relatively normal, generally "OK" human beings. If he/she is perceived otherwise, therapy is apt to become a burden and elicit little investment on the part of the client.

Furthermore, therapists must be capable of conveying a sense of humor, warmth, and understanding to their clients. Individuals engaged in marital therapy should feel comfortable with their therapists. One is best able to accomplish this by being interpersonally supportive, accepting, and sincere in his/her interaction with others. Obviously, these are not skills positively endemic to therapists alone; rather, they are behaviors that will facilitate almost all forms of social interaction. Thus, if one is to act in his/her clients' best interests, he/she must nonjudgmentally communicate respect, sensitivity, and concern. To do so allows clients to commit themselves to a proposed treatment program. Not doing so only makes the job more difficult.

*Self-disclosure.* Ample evidence exists indicating that therapist self-disclosure can be extremely useful as part of the treatment process (Bundza & Simonson, 1973; Jourard, 1968, 1971). Jourard, in particular, has emphasized that it is perfectly normal for fully actualized individuals to self-disclose. Indeed, both with respect to content and process issues, therapist self-disclosure may be highly facilitative of treatment gains. As a matter of content, therapist self-disclosure may allow individuals to explore thoughts, feelings, and behavior that previously have not been closely examined. As a matter of process, therapist self-disclosure very pragmatically illustrates a communication strategy that clients simply may not have employed in the past. Further, until clients are capable of doing so, they may be incapable of love (Jourard, 1971), because the sharing of self is such an integral part of giving to others. Thus, therapists may want to model the process of self-disclosure. In addition to teaching clients how to self-disclose, such therapist behavior is apt to have a number of other bonuses associated with it:

1. increases clients' identification with therapist,
2. creates a more trusting relationship,
3. creates a more egalitarian relationship,
4. aids clients in believing that therapist can truly understand their situation.

Clearly, however, there are instances where therapist self-disclosure may be highly inappropriate. First, self-disclosure should not occur as part of one's personal aggrandizement. Rather, one discloses himself/herself to a client when he/she firmly believes that it will be of therapeutic value to the individual or couple. Second, therapist self-disclosure certainly should not create further burdens or demands upon the client (Egan, 1975). Third, self-disclosure should not occur too frequently and must be appropriately timed (Murphy & Strong, 1972). Lastly, therapist self-disclosure must not distract clients from their primary purpose in treatment —that is, to find more effective ways of dealing with one another.

## Tactical Skills of the Therapist

Interpersonal skills of the therapist create a fertile environment for therapy. Tactical skills, on the other hand, are the "rake and hoe" by which we actually till the land. Such skills are not easily developed, but without them the likelihood of change is greatly diminished. Thus, it becomes essential that therapists constantly hone and refine the clinical metastrategies they employ in the conduct of treatment. We have divided these "super" strategies into four major groupings: (a) control, (b) activity level, (c) language, and (d) building affective-behavioral bridges.

*Control.* A number of years ago, one of us (PHB) had as a therapy supervisor a most remarkable clinician. His comments, analyses, and suggestions were appealing both because of their incisiveness and simplicity. Exemplary of these was his fundamental statement regarding clients and the problems they possess: "Clients don't leave their problems outside your door—they bring them into therapy with themselves."[1] In marital therapy, this statement translates as follows: *Give couples the opportunity to display their dysfunction and undoubtedly they will.* Obviously, there are times when this can be highly instructive for the clinician. Unfortunately, there are other times when it is wholly antitherapeutic. In other words, couples can easily recreate their negative, problematic patterns of interaction both at home and in the therapist's office. Although clinicians may be interested in learning of these patterns, there is a time when they must be more interested in changing them. And, if change is to occur, the behavior will have to be controlled in some way. If the behavior is not controlled, then it will control therapy. At this point, however, we are using the term *therapy* very loosely, for when couples come in and repeatedly display their dysfunction without effective intervention on the part of the therapist, we seriously doubt whether therapy is occurring at all.

Thus, by control we are referring to guiding, directing, and influencing the flow of therapy. The antithesis to this process is "flying by the seat of one's pants." In fact, we can think of nothing more harmful to marital therapy than working without structure or control. As a beginning graduate student once remarked about a couple he was seeing in therapy, "I don't know what I'm doing in there, and they're eating me up alive." Unfortunately, his perception was accurate. Although one might, at times, be able to get away with a lack of control in individual therapy, working with couples is another story entirely. Couples have years of practice, a history of relating to one another, and routines that

[1] I will always be indebted to Carl Sipprelle, Ph.D., for this and other similar comments.

occur reflexively. Give them the opportunity to take control, and the outcome is wholly predictable—they will, and therapeutic gains will not be achieved. As a consequence, therapist control is a necessary although not sufficient condition of effective marital therapy.

Just what is meant by therapist control? We would suggest that there are four key elements. First, therapists must have a conceptualization of the couple's problem and a treatment plan that follows accordingly from that conceptualization. Second, therapist control means determining the course of therapy both within (i.e., having a planned agenda) and across (i.e., overall treatment goals) sessions. Third, control allows therapists to provide continuity from one session to the next (e.g., via the administration of homework assignments). Lastly, control does not mean inflexibility. The therapist should be able to deal with spontaneous matters that may arise (i.e., couple's agenda), yet still manage to integrate these issues into the ongoing course of therapy. In sum, therapists take control because they must. However, their control is neither malignant nor malicious. It is always couched within the framework of human-ness, respect, and understanding that we discussed earlier.

*Activity Level.* This is an extremely significant concept that has ramifications across a wide variety of marital therapy areas. In addition, therapist activity level is directly related to the control issue as presented in the previous section. Namely, to effect the control required to make therapy successful, therapists must not only take charge, they must do so quite actively. This means, of course, that the marital therapist must be prepared to move with great speed. Failure to do so will result in continuation of the dysfunctional patterns of interaction that already characterize the couple's relationship. To accomplish this, one must be mentally alert, responsive, and energetic. In essence, marital therapy is not for the tired, weak of heart, or subassertive individual. Rather, it requires a forceful, alert, almost tenacious orientation. Moreover, this dynamism is reflected in both thought and deed. That is, one may be cognitively at work attempting to understand the couple while almost simultaneously physically moving about the room as a means of utilizing some planned therapeutic strategy (see Chapter 4). In either instance, the therapist is employing elements of classic Type A behavior, always remaining in control and one step ahead of the couple.

*Language.* There are a number of relevant dimensions with respect to therapists' tactical use of language. First, verbal interventions should be succinct, precise, and to the point. Therapists simply do not want to allow their comments to be vague, diffuse, or misinterpreted. One way in which this can be facilitated is to comment only when there is something to be said. Hapless, irrelevant, long-winded remarks have no course in therapy. In fact, virtually every therapist remark should have some therapeutic purpose in mind. Second, when speaking, therapists should be crisp, clear, and salient. Therapist comments should be powerful and demanding of client attention. The greater the clarity and impact, the higher the likelihood that comments will influence client behavior and thereby influence the relationship. Third, the actual language employed should be congruent with the language of the client. Sophisticated couples receive sophisticated language, folksy couples receive folksy language, and so on. Obviously, if therapist and client do not speak the same language, there are going to be serious difficulties in communication. One final caveat: This does not mean that clients who verbally abuse, insult, and berate their partner should expect to hear similar language from the therapist. Whatever language is employed, it is always employed in the service of therapy. Insults and abuse are rarely therapeutic. Thus, with the abusive client, therapists may wish to comment upon partners' intensity of feeling as a means of aiding understanding and hopefully creating change.

*Building Affective/Behavioral Bridges.* Alexander and Parsons (1982) have discussed the notion of affect/behavior integration. They indicate that this occurs when therapists operationalize vague language and thereby create a feeling/behavior cause-and-effect model for client understanding. This is accomplished by noting the feelings that underlie behavior ("If you did X, you must have felt very Y") and the behavior that results from feelings ("You feel very Y and therefore did X"). Although we agree with this therapeutic tactic, our purpose is slightly different. Namely, the principle we espouse is that there are a variety of ways in which spouses may interpret their partner's behavior. Because any interpretation that facilitates change is potentially of vast therapeutic value, we sometimes work toward creating change by speaking about behavior. At other times, we work toward change by focusing on feelings. In either instance, we are alert to taking full advantage of therapeutic avenues that may be available to us. The affective/behavioral dimension is one very significant avenue that affords a variety of powerful therapeutic alternatives.

## Building a Working Relationship Between Partners

Perhaps the greatest paradox of marital therapy is that couples who come in for treatment, unable to get along effectively with one another, are then called upon to work collaboratively (Jacobson & Margolin, 1979) in the remediation of their problems. Clearly, the likelihood of this spontaneously occurring is not great. In fact, given that couples typically enter therapy when matters have reached a crisis-like state, one is much more apt to find anger and distrust than acceptance and cooperation.

The problem for the marital therapist becomes one of transforming accusations and cross-complaints into cooperative attempts at problem-solving and conflict resolution. We believe there are a number of generic strategies that can be implemented for just this purpose. First, our assessment program (as discussed in Chapter 3) often produces such collaboration as a natural by-product. This probably occurs for a number of reasons. The behavioral specificity that is required does not allow for continuing vague statements of dissatisfaction. Effort is made to focus upon both positive and negative aspects of the relationship. For example, history-taking by the therapist forces most clients to recognize the positive, more satisfying aspects of their union. Second, many clients come into therapy to present their case—that is, asking the therapist to serve as judge and jury and arrive at a verdict of spousal innocence or guilt. Quite simply, we refuse to be engaged in such an adversarial process, because it serves no benefit whatsoever. Instead, we resolve to understand the problem as best we can without indictment of one party or the other. In essence, our approach is to neither condemn nor blame either individual, but rather to aid the couple in effecting a more satisfying and rewarding relationship. Third, the rationale for treatment that is provided places emphasis on both our nonblaming philosophy and the need for reciprocal behavior changes. Admittedly, we find that this in and of itself is of limited utility. However, when paired with therapeutic tasks requiring that partners act in concert, the effect is then potentiated. Indeed, the couple comes to believe that we mean what we say. Fourth, our initial focus in treatment tends to be on increasing positive aspects of the relationship. Building collaboration upon a decaying foundation is a waste of effort. Consequently, we first attempt to put some trust back into the relationship by having spouses increase their level of partner-pleasing behavior. Lastly, we require some form of public commitment to change. Therapy is defined as a change process—an unwillingness, on our part, to accept the status quo. Should the couple choose to work with us, they are then choosing to at least consider, and hopefully implement, alternative ways of relating. Such a statement on their part is a public commitment to change (even if the public is limited to two individuals—partner and therapist) and a prerequisite to the actual conduct of treatment.

Obviously, other strategies exist as a means of increasing cooperative behavior in distressed relationships (see Jacobson & Margolin, 1979). In our opinion, however, there is no one tactic that invariably produces the desired effect. Instead, therapists must have at their disposal a variety of employable strategies to facilitate a positive working relationship between partners. More importantly, whatever the strategy, it must be consistently applied across both members of the relationship. If not done so, one can expect considerable resentment and resistance from one or both members of the dyad.

## UNDERSTANDING BEHAVIOR

The first conceptual tenet discussed in Chapter 1 related to the "couple as system." At that point, we indicated that a behavioral-communications model always examines spousal behavior within its relational context. That is, behavior may serve both a literal and representational purpose in the relationship. In essence, individual behavior within relationships must be examined both as behavior and as a statement about the relationship (Watzlawick, Beavin, & Jackson, 1967). Thus, behavior is afforded meaning by the context in which it occurs.

What, then, is one to do with Spouse A's problematic behavior (e.g., lateness), which occurs in the context of Spouse B? First, the therapist must collect information so that he/she can decide if the behavior is intrapsychically or interpersonally motivated. If the problem is a function of some personal process, obviously one would want to intervene with the individual. On the other hand, lateness may be a covert means by which A tells B: "I can't take care of all these household responsibilities by myself—I need your help." Clearly, the latter instance demands a relationship-based form of therapy.

As indicated earlier, it is our belief that individual behavior may be nothing more than that—behavior that has no purposeful meaning within the relationship. Spouse A may be late because he is disorganized, habitually late, without a watch, confused, incapable of telling time, and so on. In a great many instances, however, all of these reasons can be ruled out. The personal process hypothesis is then rejected. Further, if Spouse B were to request a change in A's behavior, we would expect that change should not be all that difficult. Looking rationally at the situation:

1. A does something that bothers B.
2. B requests changes in A's behavior.
3. A loves B.
4. Given these conditions, A most certainly would want to change his/her behavior so as to please B.

Obviously, this is not what typically occurs in distressed relationships. Thus, we would conclude that "lateness" holds some meaning in the relationship and perhaps serves a communicative function between partners.

Gottman, Notarius, Gonso, and Markman (1976) refer to this process as the hidden agenda. It is comprised of an issue that is rarely discussed and consequently never resolved. They indicate that there are three major types of hidden agendas, those related to:

1. "My spouse doesn't care about me" (i.e., positiveness).
2. "My spouse is not interested in me" (i.e., responsiveness).
3. "My spouse does not treat me as an equal" (i.e., status).

Wile (1981), on the other hand, suggests that partners develop patterns of relating and that problem behaviors are simply enactments of those patterns. The major patterns that he discusses are those of mutual withdrawal, mutual accusation, and demanding-withdrawal. In a relatively similar manner, Alexander and Parsons (1982) discuss the meaning of behavior by examining the outcome produced. According to their analysis, all behaviors reduce to two major themes: contact/closeness (merging) and distance/independence (separating). Our point is actually quite simple. Behavior in relationships will frequently have an interpersonal purpose. When that occurs, the job of the therapist is as follows: (a) to understand the meaning of spousal behavior, (b) to air that meaning in a nonoffensive, constructive manner, and (c) to aid partners in negotiating solutions to the real issue problems that exist. The type and number of differing hidden agendas are probably irrelevant. What is important is that they not go unattended and that they become a focus of treatment.

One final point in this section. Dealing with hidden agendas does not mean that we are in any way advocating an avoidance of overt behavioral problems. For example, "lateness" may be the behavioral manifestation of an "I need your help" hidden agenda. One can attempt to change "lateness" without ever confronting the hidden agenda, and under some circumstances, this may work quite well. However, we would never choose to work solely on the hidden agenda without translating back to the behavioral problem of "lateness." To do so seems foolish and self-defeating in the larger context of time. Obviously, the most optimal condition involves attending to both the behavioral problem and the hidden agenda. In so doing, one solves the immediate difficulty and prevents future disturbances as well.

## OBJECTIFICATION

Objectification is the principle that underlies the process of behavioral specification. Couples generally appear for treatment unable to speak the language of behavior change. What they speak instead is a language of criticism, complaint, and anger. More important, however, is the manner in which they speak this language. That is, via the use of such vague, global, generalized statements of discontent as:

- "He doesn't love me anymore."
- "I always give and she always takes—it's just not fair."
- "We don't seem to get along. Everything ends up in a fight."
- "She doesn't appreciate anything that I do."

MT-B*

Although such concepts are initially important for outlining the parameters of conflict, they must eventually be replaced with specific descriptions of pleasing and displeasing behavior. This may be extremely difficult for some individuals, whose romanticized notions of spousal behavior do not fit well with a behavioral-referent philosophy. Unfortunately, progress in marital therapy is almost precluded without such specification. Thus, it is essential that therapists aid couples in explicitly stating their desires and expectations. These well-specified positive and negative behaviors can then become targets for therapeutic change.

Although behavioral specification is generally considered a prerequisite of effective treatment, it is an absolutely essential component of systematically applied assessment programs. As will be discussed in Chapter 3, a variety of self- and spouse-report inventories are available for the operationalization of marital excesses and deficits. In addition, Bornstein and associates (Bornstein, Anton et al., 1981; Bornstein, Bach et al., 1981; Bornstein, Hickey et al., 1983) have used an interesting laboratory-based measure for the assessment of specific dysfunctions. Using an adaptation of the Inventory of Marital Conflicts (Olson & Ryder, 1970), they had couples engage in video-recorded discussions of marital problem situations. Strodtbeck's (1951) Revealed Differences Technique was employed as a means of generating conflict. Specifically, spouses read a series of brief vignettes describing problematic marital encounters. Each partner was asked to indicate who was responsible for the problem. In those situations where differences of opinion occurred, couples were then required to role-play the vignette in question. Their instructions were to discuss and attempt to resolve the conflict within a 10-minute period of time. Based upon couples' consent, presenting complaints, and retrospective ratings of videotapes, specific targets for treatment were then selected. These included such positive behaviors as agreement and problem solution (Bornstein, Anton et al., 1981) as well as negative behaviors of complain, sidetrack, and mind reading (Bornstein, Hickey et al., 1983). Thus, on the basis of this assessment strategy, a treatment plan was tailored to the idiosyncratic problems of the couple.

Interestingly, in the previous example, part of the assessment data was direct observational information. In most clinical situations, such information is generally available during intake interviews with the couple. Obviously, we will be discussing this at greater length in the next chapter. However, even at this point it is appropriate to indicate that therapists must be astute observers of couples' behavior during the initial interview. With respect to objectification, therapists will want to pay particular attention to vagueness versus specificity in clients' descriptions of both positive and negative relationship dimensions. Furthermore, it may certainly be appropriate to either comment upon or begin a specificity-shaping program with those individuals who remain vague and imprecise in their partner-directed verbal remarks. Although one may choose to limit his/her specificity interventions during the initial interview, the task cannot be delayed for long. In fact, it is clearly one of the earliest directives in the therapeutic chain of events.

## BEHAVIORAL EXCHANGE

In Chapter 1, we discussed the principle of reciprocity. At that time, we indicated that over time individuals in relationships tend to reward and punish one another at relatively equal rates. Obviously, the reciprocity principle continues to have considerable explanatory power in describing contemporary marital relationships. However, it also forms the basis for a variety of therapeutic techniques that are generally subsumed under the heading of *behavioral exchange*.

Behavioral exchange refers to those procedures that increase partners' pleasure and satisfaction in the relationship—that is, the implementation of behaviors that presumably are desired by one's partner. Although there is a wide variety of techniques that can be employed in the service of behavioral exchange, all share a number of common elements. First, as noted in the previous section, behaviors to be implemented must be objectified or pinpointed in some manner. Second, efforts must be taken to actually increase or decrease the behaviors specified above. Third, evaluation must be conducted to see what effect behavioral exchange has had upon the relationship. In sum, these procedures provide a systematic means for mutually administered increases in partner-experienced relationship satisfaction.

The vast majority of couples enter therapy with a host of partner-related complaints. In fact, the marital research generally indicates that negative behaviors are more salient than positive behaviors in determining overall level of marital satisfaction (Wills et al., 1974). *However, our tendency is to initially identify and attempt to increase partner-administered positive exchanges.* There is a variety of reasons for this approach. First, increasing positive behaviors is a relatively simple, low-cost procedure. It may not require enormous effort on the part of spouses, yet the payoff may be considerable. Second, positive exchange is apt to provide partners with a marital success experience. We can think of no better way to create a therapeutic halo effect than through such a process. Third, couples need to recognize that their partners can provide them with pleasurable experiences and rewarding opportunities, and that, in fact, there may be something to be gained from continuing in the relationship. Lastly, there is some empirical support for the notion that negative behaviors may decrease as a result of therapy, even when they are not the primary focus of treatment (Margolin & Weiss, 1978). Thus, it may not be necessary to directly attack all negative forms of interaction, especially early in therapy.

When successful, the effect of initially working on positive exchanges can be enormously powerful. Spouses recognize that there are alternatives to continued hostility and distrust. Instead, they re-experience the positive aspects of the relationship that may have been buried for some time. This, in itself, is clearly of merit. Additionally, however, positive exchange provides couples with the necessary incentive to continue their efforts at reconciliation. In those instances where therapists must eventually focus on negative behaviors, the positive exchange procedure provides a firm foundation for later therapeutic interventions. In fact, our experience indicates that this will be required in the vast majority of instances. Given that a small reduction in the rate of negative interactions may lead to a sizable increase in marital satisfaction (Bornstein, Hickey et al., 1983), it would certainly appear to be a judicious investment of therapeutic time to attend to both positive and negative exchange. Exactly how this might be accomplished will be discussed in Chapter 4.

## COMPROMISE

Although there are those who would argue against continuing compromise in marriage (Wile, 1981), our position is that compromise plays a very significant role in resolving marital disputes and increasing partner satisfaction. Under normal circumstances, most married people get along with one another just fine, but they run into problems when their desires come into conflict with one another. For example, John wants to stay at home and watch a televised Sunday afternoon football game; Mary wants to have a picnic and walk around a nearby state park. It is obvious that both partners' desires cannot be accomplished at the exact same time. Therefore, either John "wins," Mary "wins," or some equitable compromise is reached. We would go so far as to state that if either partner consistently "wins," then the relationship consistently "loses." If compromise over time can be achieved, however, then everyone (John, Mary, and the relationship) ends up big "winners."

The chapter on problem-solving (Chapter 6) will discuss in detail exactly how this is accomplished. At this point, we would like to simply note that successful marriage, *by necessity*, must involve some sort of sacrifice and compromise. Two people cannot live together as one. That is another of those false expectations that has been foisted upon people as part of the romantic ideal. There will be areas of disagreement and dispute. Ideally, most individuals would like to settle these disputes by having their way. To do so, however, will only serve to alienate and further distance partners from one another. As a consequence, it becomes therapeutically advisable to train couples in the art of compromise. This does not mean that partners must always be prepared to renounce or forgo their personal desires. Rather, compromise entails perhaps adjusting one's personal desires in light of one's partner's desires. Those incapable of accomplishing this are those who want to get, but are unwilling to give. Quite frankly, they make lousy marital partners.

## SUMMARY

Five major principles of relationship change were presented in this chapter: (a) creating a positive working relationship, (b) understanding behavior, (c) objectification, (d) behavioral exchange, and (e) compromise. Developing a positive working relationship was examined from the perspective of interpersonal skills of the therapist, tactical skills of the therapist, and collaboration between marital partners. To change dysfunctional behavior within relationships, it was recommended that therapists always consider behavior within its relational context (i.e., both the intra- and interpersonal meaning of behavior). In all instances, the specification of behavior affords one the opportunity to systematically intervene within distressed relationships. A major way in which this is accomplished is through behavioral exchange techniques and problem-solving strategies. Compromise is envisioned as a primary component of most problem-solving/conflict resolution programs.

# Chapter 3
# The Assessment of Marital Interaction*

The assessment of marital interaction provides information that is central both to the understanding and treatment of intimate relationships. Quite simply, a comprehensive assessment will dictate the focus of treatment (Bornstein, Bornstein, & Dawson, 1984). Indeed, the systematic measurement of marital interaction should not only improve treatment effectiveness, but also provide an empirical basis for the evaluation of therapeutic efficacy. This chapter examines a variety of assessment strategies that offer useful clinical information, while remaining realistic and practical (Nelson, 1981) in administration time. To accomplish this, we will first discuss the intake interview and then direct our attention to more specific marital assessment instruments. From a behavioral-communications perspective, the intake interview represents a point of departure both in terms of marital assessment and treatment.

## INTAKE INTERVIEWING STRATEGIES

### Purpose

The intake interview attempts to accomplish three primary functions: (a) development of a therapeutic working relationship, (b) collection of assessment information, and (c) implementation of initial therapeutic regimes. Because spouses entering treatment often have spent months, if not years, in conflict and distress, the intake interview provides clinicians with a unique opportunity to immediately impact and assess the couple's system. In fact, the initial interview may be the single most important session in all conjoint marital therapy. In addition to the primary functions listed previously, effective intake interviews will also typically create pos-

*This chapter was co-authored by Gregory L. Wilson.

itive expectancies for change. Obviously, such expectations can be of great initial significance.

Because distressed couples often devote a considerable amount of time to thinking about and engaging in conflicted and discordant relations, it naturally follows that they will attempt to engage in "negative tracking" during the initial interview. Although information regarding current difficulties and concerns is clearly valuable, nonconflicted, positive forms of tracking may be of even greater merit. Thus, interventions designed to modify ongoing, faulty patterns of interaction actually begin during the first session.

Whereas all relationships include both positive and negative dimensions, distressed couples typically fail to recognize the continuing positive aspects of their marital situation. Thus, couples must be encouraged to explore the varying facets of their relationships. In so doing, clinicians disrupt negative tracking and provide opportunity to observe a variety of marital interaction forms. Besides acknowledging the reinforcing behaviors that remain in the relationship, positive tracking will often generate some feelings of hope. Moreover, by commenting on reciprocity and positive control strategies, the therapist may immediately promote their continued application in extra-therapy settings.

The initial interview also enables clients to discover what *you* and *therapy* are all about. Thus, assessment occurs on a variety of levels. The therapist's style, behavior, and general approach to treatment are clearly being evaluated. As a consequence, clinicians must be somewhat cautious during their initial contact. At this point, there is considerable likelihood of miscommunication, misunderstanding, and misperception. Given the nature of this first meeting, therapists must therefore be extremely watchful of client potential misconstructions.

## Tasks

As described in Chapter 2, the establishment of an effective working relationship is essential to the therapeutic transaction. During intake, the therapist's interpersonal style may well represent the most critical component in this formative process. Of particular import is the therapist's ability to appear calm, confident, and competent. Because most couples seeking therapy are confused and apprehensive about engaging in treatment (Jacobson & Margolin, 1979), the therapist's ability to allay client anxiety and appear "in control" is essential to successful intake interviews.

*Opening Remarks.* Therapists should begin by providing a brief statement regarding the format and purpose of the initial session.

> *Therapist: (following initial greetings and introductions)* Let me just fill you in
> a little bit on what we'll be doing today. As you already know, we'll be
> meeting until four o'clock. In the time that we have, I'd like to get to know
> you individually and as a couple. I'll be asking you a number of ques-
> tions both about your current and past situation. My general purpose
> is to better understand your relationship and see if I can be of service
> to you. Okay?
> *Wife:* Fine.
> *Therapist:* Good, then where would you like to begin?

These very simple comments are intended to allay client anxiety and provide initial information. The calm, controlled, orderly approach to treatment has already begun. The therapist can now sit back for a moment and
observe the couple's response to his/her introductory remarks. Undoubtedly, one can expect that a couple's statement of presenting complaint
is soon to follow.

*Presenting Problems.* Providing an initial open-ended question, as indicated
in the previous discussion, is actually an invitation for information. Unfortunately, a great many couples do not accept this invitation in a productive manner. Instead, they may immediately become vague, accusing,
nonverbal, dominating, or hostile. In any case, they are providing the
clinician with significant assessment "data." However, once these "data"
have been obtained, the couple's negative interaction is apt to be of limited
value. Thus, the therapist will want to redirect the interaction through continued information gathering. This will usually take the form of behaviorally specific questions and inquiries. Appropriate questions at this time
may include any of the following:

1. Who initiated contact with the therapist?
2. What factors precipitated the decision to seek possible treatment at this
   time?
3. Has the couple ever sought treatment in the past?
4. How long have such problems existed?
5. What has the couple done to control such problems in the past?
6. What does the couple see as the goals of therapy?

Furthermore, it is important to note several aspects of the couple's interaction at this time. For example: To what degree do both partners participate
in providing relevant information? Do partners play the role of victim and
victimizer? Are the partner's interactions complimentary or oppositional?
What does one spouse do while the other speaks? What changes are evident in the couple's verbal and nonverbal behavior when one spouse
becomes irritated or upset? Besides identifying reluctant therapy candi-
dates, attention to these issues begins to highlight the couple's idiosyn-

cratic relationship rules and roles that may serve to maintain or exacerbate their current difficulties.

Encouraging both partners to engage in direct discussion with each other further enables the clinician to begin assessing communication skills and problem-solving abilities. However, during such interactions, the therapist must be careful not to align himself/herself with either partner. Instead, the intake interview must provide information without the therapist appearing to have accepted one partner's definition of the problem. Moreover, if one partner has reservations about entering treatment, this too should be accepted as a credible position. Consequently, such reservations should be discussed and employed as part of the therapeutic process.

*Developmental History.* Immediately following a relatively brief description of the couple's relationship difficulties, a gathering of historical information is usually in order. From an assessment perspective, developmental history enables the therapist to better understand the present marital situation in light of the couple's previous experience together. Therapeutically, attention is shifted away from current sources of distress and refocused on earlier events in the relationship. This tends to have an immediately positive effect. Specific topics that should be of historical developmental interest include:

1. *First Meetings*
   When did you first meet?
   How did you get to know each other?
   What attracted you to one another?
2. *Courtship*
   When did you begin dating?
   What kinds of things did you do together?
   What do you remember best of those early days together?
   Were there any special things or times together that
       stand out in your memory (e.g., first date, first
       sexual encounter, weekend together, etc.)?
   What led you to decide to marry (or live together)?
   Were other factors (e.g., pregnancy, parental pressure,
       etc.) involved in your decision to marry (or live
       together)?
3. *Marriage and Early Years*
   What was your wedding like?
   Did you have a honeymoon?
   What were your expectations about the future?
   As you look back on your relationship, how would you
       describe your early years together?

What kinds of things did you do for fun?
How did you handle conflicts and disagreements then?
4. *Most Recent Period*
What's happened to make things different?
Have things changed abruptly or slowly over time?
What do you think the prospects are for the future?

Additional developmental concerns include: brief personal histories, family histories (i.e., emphasizing early marital models and family interaction), and previous therapy experience. If there has been some period of time between referral and initial appointment, it is also wise to inquire as to how the relationship has changed since contacting the therapist.

*Cross-sectional History.* In addition to collecting developmental history, therapists should gather cross-sectional information as well. Such data are most efficiently garnered by asking couples to describe a typical day. Particular attention should be focused on both the specific content and manner in which spouses describe their interactions. Cross-sectional histories also provide the therapist with information relative to current marital costs and benefits. Issues of greatest concern here tend to include: amount of time together, quality of time together, level of shared activities, third-party involvements, acts of consideration, and so on. In sum, a cross-sectional history should provide the clinician with a much fuller sense of how the present marital situation is actually experienced by each partner in the relationship.

*Initial Intervention.* By the conclusion of the initial interview, the therapist will have gathered a considerable amount of assessment information. Moreover, each spouse should be feeling more comfortable and relaxed about therapy, per se. In some cases, this may not be enough, and individuals may need a more concrete sense of just what can be accomplished in treatment. As a consequence, quite frequently, we will purposefully attempt to deal with a relatively minor issue sometime during the initial session. Our intention here is quite clear—to demonstrate that positive effects can be achieved as a result of therapy. The therapist should be certain, however, to choose a problem that he/she understands and that can, in fact, be resolved in an expeditious manner. Once again, the point is to turn the couple on to treatment. Choosing a problem that cannot be effectively resolved is apt to have dire consequences for the continuation of therapy. Thus, one must have a very clear sense that the chosen problem is within the range of immediate treatability. We are reminded of a recent example where a husband failed to put the newspaper away after reading it each evening. This was upsetting to his wife for a variety of reasons. Most significant, however, was that she found it to be a highly inconsiderate act—a demonstration of the husband's lack of concern for her. Once this became clear, during the initial session, the opportunity for resolution was evident. Namely, the husband's intention was not to act in an inconsiderate manner. His statements appeared quite genuine, and as a consequence, we initiated an intervention to modify the behavior. Under therapist direction, the husband and wife discussed the matter and very reasonably settled the argument. Moreover, a homework assignment was provided relevant to the issue at hand. Thus, at the close of the initial intake session, not only had the matter been resolved, but some generalization had already been programmed to the natural environment. Obviously, this cannot always be accomplished. However, when possible, therapists should feel free to take advantage of such opportunities.

*Closing Remarks.* As the initial session ends, the therapist should have a developing sense of how the couple relates to one another. A variety of issues will have been addressed, therapeutic relationships initially formed, and first-order interventions perhaps already established. Yet, there are a number of other matters still to be accomplished.

First, the therapist should attempt to provide limited feedback with regard to the marital situation. Typically, this can best be accomplished by: (a) summarizing the session, (b) highlighting each spouse's concerns, (c) noting the goals discussed, and (d) commenting upon the couple's interactional style. The purpose is not to supply definitive feedback, but rather to provide some degree of closure. In that regard, couples should be told how many further assessment sessions will be required (usually one to two) and what fees for service they will incur. Second, couples must be informed as to whether the initial intake session is representative of future meetings. In general, this is typically the case; that is, individuals will be encouraged to talk directly to one another, complete homework as assigned, and so on. Third, the therapist should receive a commitment from both individuals that they are willing to complete the two- to three-session assessment sequence. Upon receiving that commitment, take-home paper-and-pencil instruments should be distributed and dates arranged for the final assessment meetings.

Once all assessment sessions have been completed, significantly more detailed information should be provided to clients. This entails the following:

1. feedback regarding marital strengths and weaknesses
2. explanation and rationale for the treatment process (Bornstein, Fox et al., 1983)

3. goals of therapy
4. estimated number of meetings required (90% of all cases can be completed within 12 sessions)
5. discussion of fees and payment schedule
6. "ground rules" of treatment.

All of the items in this list are presented in a collaborative manner. Thus, for example, the therapist should never dogmatically "tell" the clients what they must change about themselves or the relationship. Rather, treatment plans should be presented as a suggested course of action to be approved by all parties concerned. Further, misconceptions with respect to the overall goals of treatment must be allayed. The purpose of treatment is not to "save this marriage," but rather to aid participants in reaching decisions regarding what is best for them as individuals and as a couple.

Before asking couples to commit themselves to treatment, they must also be informed as to the "ground rules" of therapy. These are quite simple and typically can be explained in a very matter-of-fact manner. First, individual contacts between client and clinician outside of therapy are discouraged. Although such contact may be necessary, it is best accomplished in the presence of all parties involved in the therapy. Thus, if individual contact (e.g., private phone calls) occurs, the therapist will feel free to discuss the nature of that contact with everyone present at the next therapy meeting. Second, extramarital affairs must be terminated during the course of treatment. Therapy requires a commitment to work, and an extramarital relationship simply serves as an obstacle to the successful completion of that work. Third, spouses must agree that no retribution occurs outside of therapy for information disclosed during session. Fourth, all information discussed in therapy must be kept confidential. Clearly, there are therapist limits to this confidentiality. For example, abusive acts or threats of violence will not be condoned, and appropriate legal measures will be taken. Finally, couples should be informed that when homework is assigned and agreed to, it is expected to be completed.

At the close of the assessment period, two final steps remain: (a) whether there are any questions, and whether the couple wants to enter treatment. Obviously, the therapist should answer all questions as clearly and honestly as possible. The latter issue, however, can be dealt with in a slightly more strategic manner. Specifically, we ask that couples reach a mutual decision about therapy by engaging in private discussion. That is, they are to go home, discuss the matter fully, and then recontact us with their decision. By refusing to accept even an affirmative decision offered during the session, couples are, in essence, required to begin the collaborative process. Furthermore, under these circumstances, spouses are less likely to feel coerced into treatment. In sum, successful assessment interviews lay the foundation for effective treatment. The format utilized is efficient yet flexible enough to account for differences in therapist interpersonal style. Moreover, the vast array of formal instruments available beyond clinical interview affords even greater individual latitude. As a consequence, let us now examine those instruments and general measurement strategies.

## MARITAL ASSESSMENT INSTRUMENTS AND MEASUREMENT STRATEGIES

Numerous assessment instruments and measurement procedures have been developed in order to better understand intimate relationships. As described in Chapter 1, many of these assessments have been used primarily to differentiate between distressed and nondistressed couples. Although the instruments are highly informative, many have been promulgated with little regard to clinical applicability (Margolin, 1981). The following section highlights assessment strategies that not only provide useful data about marital interaction, but also represent realistic and practical methods of measurement.

To begin, marital measures, like all assessments, can be evaluated along a variety of dimensions. In searching for appropriate instruments, clinicians need to ask themselves several specific questions. For example:

1. What are the relative benefits associated with using these measures?
2. To what degree is the specific information gathered by these measures potentially useful?
   - How reliable is the information gathered by these measures?
   - How valid is the information gathered by these measures?
   - How well do these measures assess distress and satisfaction in relationships?
   - How well do these measures assess specific components (e.g., communication skills) of the marital system?
   - How well do the results from these measures lead to potential interventions?
   - How well do the results indicate whether or not treatment interventions should be modified or discontinued?
   - To what degree may these measures promote constructive change in the relationship?
   - How well do these measures assess treatment outcome effectiveness?

Whereas the preceding questions focus primarily on the potential bene-fits associated with assessment strategies, practitioners may want to ad-dress a variety of other factors before selecting measurement instruments. For example:

1. What are the relative costs associated with using these measures?
2. To what degree is the specific information gathered by these measures overshadowed by other concerns?
   - What is required of the client in order to complete these measures?
   - How much time is needed to administer, score, and interpret these measures?
   - What additional equipment, facilities, or personnel are needed to administer, score, and interpret these measures?
   - When should these measures be administered?

Based on the preceding factors, all assessment strategies differ in terms of their applicability and appropriateness for any given couple. Therefore, individually tailoring the measurement package is the most prudent and practical course of action. However, before examining a variety of specific instruments, let us present an overview of the marital assessment process.

## Overview

Unlike those instruments designed for use with individual clients, meas-ures of marital interaction attempt to assess at least three different but in-terdependent systems: (a) husband, (b) wife, and (c) marital system itself (Lederer & Jackson, 1968). Issues become more complex as one considers that the couple exists in relation to other systems, such as the immediate family, extended family, and community-at-large (Margolin, 1981). Be-cause each spouse is constantly influencing and being influenced by the other's behavior, it is inadvisable to apply standard assessment strategies solely to each partner without also evaluating the couple's interaction within the marital system.

In order to design and conduct comprehensive marital assessments, the following factors should be taken into consideration. The measurement battery should:

1. evaluate a variety of relationship dimensions (e.g., communication skills, problem-solving abilities, etc.)
2. include measures that can be used both in the natural environment and in the therapy setting
3. gather subjective (e.g., self-reports) and objective data (e.g., behavioral-ly referenced information) about the relationship

4. include measures to be employed at regular intervals (e.g., pre-, post-, follow-up) and continuously throughout treatment
5. evaluate couples' interactions along three primary response modes: (a) self-report, (b) spouse-report, and (c) external-observer report.

Table 3.1 lists common assessment instruments as a function of their primary response mode. Whereas detailed information about these instruments and other assessment methods may be found elsewhere (e.g., Filsinger & Lewis, 1981; Jacobson, 1981; Jacobson, Elwood, & Dallas, 1981; Jacobson & Margolin, 1979; Margolin & Jacobson, 1981), brief descriptions of each instrument are presented in this chapter. First, however, a closer examination of the three primary response modes is offered.

## Response Modes

Assessment of marital interaction can occur from a variety of perspectives (Markman, Notarius, Stephen, & Smith, 1981). Whereas others (e.g., Jacobson & Margolin, 1979; Olson, 1978; Weiss & Margolin, 1977) have developed similar multidimensional programs, the three primary response modes considered here include: (a) self-report, (b) spouse-report, and (c) external-observer report (i.e., those instruments designed to assess marital interaction that are completed by "others" such as trained/untrained observers, significant others, or therapists).

Self-report measures play a central role in the assessment of marital distress. By definition, relationship satisfaction or dissatisfaction is de-

Table 3.1. Common Assessment Instruments as a Function of Primary Response Mode

| Assessment Instrument | Primary Response Mode | | |
| --- | --- | --- | --- |
| | Self- | Spouse- | External-Observer |
| Dyadic Adjustment Scale (and Locke-Wallace Marital Adjustment Scale) | X | | |
| Marital Happiness Scale | X | | |
| Marital Satisfaction Time Line | X | | |
| Client Satisfaction Questionnaire | X | | |
| Marital Satisfaction Inventory | X | X | |
| Marital Observation Checklist (and Spouse Observation Checklist) | X | X | |
| Primary Communication Inventory | X | X | |
| Marital Interaction Coding System | | | X |
| Couples Interaction Scoring System | | | X |
| Verbal Problem Checklist | | | X |

pendent upon each spouse's appraisal or perception of the relationship. Although self-report is vulnerable to distortion and bias, some questionnaires and instruments can significantly aid marital therapists in understanding the couple (Jacobson et al., 1981). Specifically, these measures address questions that are critical in the formulation, implementation, and evaluation of treatment interventions. Moreover, self-report assessment strategies are inexpensive, cost-efficient, easy to administer/score, and often promote positive changes in the marital relationship.

Spouse-report instruments provide highly valuable, yet potentially unreliable information. On the one hand, spouses are uniquely qualified to observe and report on all aspects of marital interaction. In addition, marital partners represent highly efficient and practical sources of information. However, high levels of reactivity and bias are inherent in the spouse's dual role as participant and observer (see Jacobson et al., 1981; Weiss & Margolin, 1977). Thus, data obtained from spouse-report instruments must be carefully evaluated against a background of other assessment information. Interestingly, biased or "inaccurate" information, when uncovered, represents significant data, in itself, about the couple and their interactions.

In contrast to self- and spouse-reports, most external-observer reports provide unbiased, behaviorally based data about marital relationships. Within the last decade, several observational systems designed to assess couples' interactions have been shown to reliably differentiate distressed and nondistressed couples. In addition, the application of such methods to intimate relationships has provided for the systematic and quantifiable study of marital interaction. Proponents of behavioral observation systems further argue that "Studying what people say about themselves is no substitute for studying how they behave. . . . We need to look at what people do with one another" (Raush, Barry, Hertel, & Swain, 1974, p. 5). Unfortunately, most clinicians do not have adequate personnel, equipment, or resources necessary for direct observation (Jacobson et al., 1981). Thus, the applicability of such assessment strategies in clinical practice is minimal and restricted.

## Specific Assessment Instruments

*Dyadic Adjustment Scale and Locke-Wallace Marital Adjustment Scale.* The Dyadic Adjustment Scale (DAS; Spanier, 1976; see Table 3.2) and the Locke-Wallace Marital Adjustment Scale (MAS; Locke & Wallace, 1959) are two widely used self-report questionnaires that provide global indexes of marital distress. Both instruments elicit subjective impressions regarding degree of satisfaction. Reliability and validity studies on both scales are consistently positive. In fact, Spanier (1976) reports an internal consistency of $r = .96$ and substantial criterion-related validity with the more frequently used and recently developed DAS. Furthermore, factor analysis of the DAS has resulted in four components of adjustment: (a) dyadic satisfaction, (b) dyadic cohesion, (c) dyadic consensus, and (d) affectional expression. Additional advantages of both scales include ease of administration, high stability over time, and well-established norms. Based on these factors, the DAS and MAS are frequently employed as screening devices to differentiate between satisfied and dissatisfied couples. Wherever possible, we recommend using the DAS due to its psychometric sophistication (compared to the MAS) and applicability with unmarried, cohabitating couples.

*Marital Happiness Scale.* The Marital Happiness Scale (MHS; Azrin, Naster, & Jones, 1973), as modified by Bornstein and his colleagues (Bornstein, Wilson et al., 1984; Bornstein, Wilson et al., 1985), provides a rapid assessment of 11 common areas of marital interaction: (a) household responsibilities, (b) rearing of children, (c) social activities, (d) money, (e) communication, (f) sex, (g) academic (or occupational) progress, (h) personal independence, (i) partner independence, (j) affection, and (k) general happiness. Spouses rate their degree of marital happiness on a scale of 1-10 for each component of interaction (see Table 3.3). Scores on the MHS can be quickly calculated and interpreted, thereby providing almost instantaneous feedback for couples.

*Marital Satisfaction Time Line.* The Marital Satisfaction Time Line (MSTL; Williams, 1979) was developed as an assessment procedure that: (a) could be used in the natural environment, (b) would not require outside observers, and (c) would provide a highly cost-efficient measure of relationship satisfaction. The MSTL accomplishes all of these, both with regard to quantity and quality of marital interaction. In using the instrument, spouses record, on a daily basis, the amount of time spent together and an overall satisfaction rating using a 10-point Likert scale. Previous research (e.g., Williams, 1979) has shown that MSTL data differentiate distressed and nondistressed couples on the basis of: (a) marital interaction quantity, (b) quality ratings of interaction intervals, (c) ratio of positive to negative time, and (d) amount of spousal agreement regarding quality of time.

*Client Satisfaction Questionnaire.* The Client Satisfaction Questionnaire (CSQ; Larsen, Attkisson, Hargreaves, & Nguyen, 1979) is a direct, practical, and highly cost-efficient means of evaluating clients' evaluation of services provided (see Table 3.4). Although not developed specifically to assess clients' response to marital therapy per se, the CSQ provides a

Table 3.2. Dyadic Adjustment Scale

Most persons have disagreements in their relationships. Please indicate below the approximate extent of agreement or disagreement between you and your partner for each item on the following list.

| | Always agree | Almost always agree | Occasionally disagree | Frequently disagree | Almost always disagree | Always disagree |
|---|---|---|---|---|---|---|
| 1. Handling family finances | 5 | 4 | 3 | 2 | 1 | 0 |
| 2. Matters of recreation | 5 | 4 | 3 | 2 | 1 | 0 |
| 3. Religious matters | 5 | 4 | 3 | 2 | 1 | 0 |
| 4. Demonstrations of affection | 5 | 4 | 3 | 2 | 1 | 0 |
| 5. Friends | 5 | 4 | 3 | 2 | 1 | 0 |
| 6. Sex relations | 5 | 4 | 3 | 2 | 1 | 0 |
| 7. Conventionality (correct or proper behavior) | 5 | 4 | 3 | 2 | 1 | 0 |
| 8. Philosophy of life | 5 | 4 | 3 | 2 | 1 | 0 |
| 9. Ways of dealing with parents or in-laws | 5 | 4 | 3 | 2 | 1 | 0 |
| 10. Aims, goals, and things believed important | 5 | 4 | 3 | 2 | 1 | 0 |
| 11. Amount of time spent together | 5 | 4 | 3 | 2 | 1 | 0 |
| 12. Making major decisions | 5 | 4 | 3 | 2 | 1 | 0 |
| 13. Household tasks | 5 | 4 | 3 | 2 | 1 | 0 |
| 14. Leisure-time interests and activities | 5 | 4 | 3 | 2 | 1 | 0 |
| 15. Career decisions | 5 | 4 | 3 | 2 | 1 | 0 |

| | All the time | Most of the time | More often than not | Occasionally | Rarely | Never |
|---|---|---|---|---|---|---|
| 16. How often do you discuss or have you considered divorce, separation, or terminating your relationship? | 0 | 1 | 2 | 3 | 4 | 5 |
| 17. How often do you or your mate leave the house after a fight? | 0 | 1 | 2 | 3 | 4 | 5 |
| 18. In general, how often do you think that things between you and your partner are going well? | 5 | 4 | 3 | 2 | 1 | 0 |
| 19. Do you confide in your mate? | 5 | 4 | 3 | 2 | 1 | 0 |
| 20. Do you ever regret that you married (or lived together)? | 0 | 1 | 2 | 3 | 4 | 5 |
| 21. How often do you and your partner quarrel? | 0 | 1 | 2 | 3 | 4 | 5 |
| 22. How often do you and your mate "get on each other's nerves"? | 0 | 1 | 2 | 3 | 4 | 5 |

| | Every day | Almost Every day | Occasionally | Rarely | Never |
|---|---|---|---|---|---|
| 23. Do you kiss your mate? | | | | | |

24. Do you and your mate engage in outside interests together?

| | All of them | Most of them | Some of them | Very few of them | None of them |
|---|---|---|---|---|---|
| | 4 | 3 | 2 | 1 | 0 |

How often would you say the following occur between you and your mate:

| | Never | Less than once a month | Once or twice a month | Once or twice a week | Once a day | More often |
|---|---|---|---|---|---|---|
| | | 1 | 2 | 3 | 4 | 5 |
| 25. Have a stimulating exchange of ideas | 0 | 1 | 2 | 3 | 4 | 5 |
| 26. Laugh together | 0 | 1 | 2 | 3 | 4 | 5 |
| 27. Calmly discuss something | 0 | 1 | 2 | 3 | 4 | 5 |
| 28. Work together on a project | 0 | 1 | 2 | 3 | 4 | 5 |

These are some things about which couples sometimes agree and sometimes disagree. Indicate if either item below caused differences of opinions or were problems in your relationship during the past few weeks. (Check yes or no.)

| | Yes | No |
|---|---|---|
| 29. Being too tired for sex | 0 | 1 |
| 30. Not showing love | 0 | 1 |

31. The dots on the following line represent different degrees of happiness in your relationship. The point, "happy," represents the degree of happiness of most relationships. Please circle the dot that best describes the degree of happiness, all things considered, of your relationship.

| 0 | 1 | 2 | 3 | 4 | 5 | 6 |
|---|---|---|---|---|---|---|
| • | • | • | • | • | • | • |
| Extremely unhappy | Fairly unhappy | A little unhappy | Happy | Very happy | Extremely happy | Perfect |

32. Which of the following statements best describes how you feel about the future of your relationship:

5    I want desperately for my relationship to succeed and would go to almost any lengths to see that it does.

4    I want very much for my relationship to succeed and will do all that I can to see that it does.

3    I want very much for my relationship to succeed and will do my fair share to see that it does.

2    It would be nice if my relationship succeeded, and I can't do much more than I am doing now to help it succeed.

1    It would be nice if it succeeded, but I refuse to do any more than I am doing now to keep the relationship going.

0    My relationship can never succeed, and there is no more that I can do to keep the relationship going.

*Note:* From "The Dyadic Adjustment Scale by Spanier," by Graham B. Spanier, 1976, *Journal of Marriage and the Family, 38,* pp. 15–28. Copyright 1976 by the National Council on Family Relations, 1910 West County Road, Suite 147, St. Paul, MN 55113. Reprinted with permission.

Table 3.3. Marital Happiness Scale

| | Completely unhappy | | | | | | | Completely happy | | |
|---|---|---|---|---|---|---|---|---|---|---|
| Household responsibilities | 1 | 2 | 3 | 4 | 5 | 6 | 7 | 8 | 9 | 10 |
| Rearing of children | 1 | 2 | 3 | 4 | 5 | 6 | 7 | 8 | 9 | 10 |
| Social activities | 1 | 2 | 3 | 4 | 5 | 6 | 7 | 8 | 9 | 10 |
| Money | 1 | 2 | 3 | 4 | 5 | 6 | 7 | 8 | 9 | 10 |
| Communication | 1 | 2 | 3 | 4 | 5 | 6 | 7 | 8 | 9 | 10 |
| Sex | 1 | 2 | 3 | 4 | 5 | 6 | 7 | 8 | 9 | 10 |
| Academic (or occupational) progress | 1 | 2 | 3 | 4 | 5 | 6 | 7 | 8 | 9 | 10 |
| Personal independence | 1 | 2 | 3 | 4 | 5 | 6 | 7 | 8 | 9 | 10 |
| Partner independence | 1 | 2 | 3 | 4 | 5 | 6 | 7 | 8 | 9 | 10 |
| Affection | 1 | 2 | 3 | 4 | 5 | 6 | 7 | 8 | 9 | 10 |
| General happiness | 1 | 2 | 3 | 4 | 5 | 6 | 7 | 8 | 9 | 10 |

Note: This scale is intended to estimate your *current* happiness with your relationship on each of the 11 dimensions listed. You are to circle one of the numbers (1–10) beside each area. Numbers toward the left end of the 10-unit scale indicate some degree of unhappiness, and numbers toward the right end of the scale reflect varying degrees of happiness. Ask yourself this question as you rate each area: "If my partner continues to act in the future as he (she) acted during the past week with respect to this area, how happy will I be *with this area of our relationship?*" In other words, state according to the numerical scale (1–10) exactly how you feel today about the past week. Try to exclude all feelings from other weeks and concentrate only on the feelings you have about the week you and your partner just spent together. Also, try not to allow one category to influence the results of the other categories.

Note: From "The Marital Happiness Scale" by N. H. Azrin, B. J. Naster and R. Jones, 1973, *Behaviour Research and Therapy, 11,* pp. 365–382. Copyright 1973 by Pergamon Press, Ltd. Used with permission.

general measure of satisfaction that can be used to evaluate the acceptability of a marital treatment program. In addition, the CSQ is a simple scale to administer, with sound psychometric properties, and requires no more than 5 minutes to complete. Scores on the CSQ range from 8 to 32, with higher scores indicative of greater treatment acceptability/satisfaction. Bornstein and Rychtarik (1983) suggest that it is the instrument of choice in contemporary program evaluation research.

*Marital Satisfaction Inventory.* The Marital Satisfaction Inventory (MSI; Snyder, 1979a) is a comprehensive, psychometrically sound self-report and spouse-report instrument containing both global and specific measures of marital interaction. The MSI contains 280 true-false items divided into 11 nonoverlapping scales: (a) conventionalization, (b) global distress, (c) affective communication, (d) problem-solving communication, (e) time together, (f) disagreement about finances, (g) sexual dissatisfaction, (h) role orientation, (i) family history of distress, (j) dissatisfaction with children, and (k) conflict over childrearing. Various studies have confirmed the reliability and validity of the MSI (e.g., Berg & Snyder, 1981; Snyder, 1979b; Snyder, 1981). Clearly, the MSI represents an extremely useful marital measure that is also helpful in formulating differential treatment plans (Wills & Snyder, 1982).

Table 3.4. The Client Satisfaction Questionnaire (CSQ)

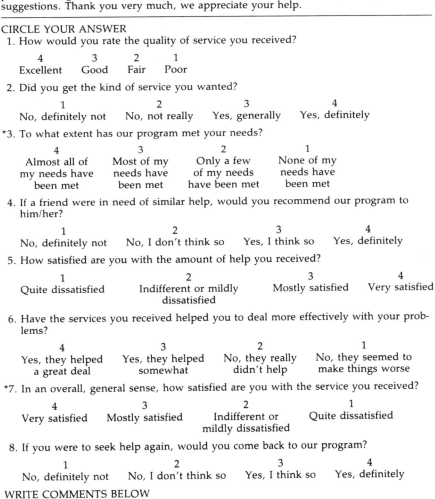

Please help us improve our program by answering some questions about the services you have received at the _____. We are interested in your honest opinions, whether they are positive or negative. *Please answer all of the questions.* We also welcome your comments and suggestions. Thank you very much, we appreciate your help.

CIRCLE YOUR ANSWER

1. How would you rate the quality of service you received?

| 4 | 3 | 2 | 1 |
|---|---|---|---|
| Excellent | Good | Fair | Poor |

2. Did you get the kind of service you wanted?

| 1 | 2 | 3 | 4 |
|---|---|---|---|
| No, definitely not | No, not really | Yes, generally | Yes, definitely |

*3. To what extent has our program met your needs?

| 4 | 3 | 2 | 1 |
|---|---|---|---|
| Almost all of my needs have been met | Most of my needs have been met | Only a few of my needs have been met | None of my needs have been met |

4. If a friend were in need of similar help, would you recommend our program to him/her?

| 1 | 2 | 3 | 4 |
|---|---|---|---|
| No, definitely not | No, I don't think so | Yes, I think so | Yes, definitely |

5. How satisfied are you with the amount of help you received?

| 1 | 2 | 3 | 4 |
|---|---|---|---|
| Quite dissatisfied | Indifferent or mildly dissatisfied | Mostly satisfied | Very satisfied |

6. Have the services you received helped you to deal more effectively with your problems?

| 4 | 3 | 2 | 1 |
|---|---|---|---|
| Yes, they helped a great deal | Yes, they helped somewhat | No, they really didn't help | No, they seemed to make things worse |

*7. In an overall, general sense, how satisfied are you with the service you received?

| 4 | 3 | 2 | 1 |
|---|---|---|---|
| Very satisfied | Mostly satisfied | Indifferent or mildly dissatisfied | Quite dissatisfied |

8. If you were to seek help again, would you come back to our program?

| 1 | 2 | 3 | 4 |
|---|---|---|---|
| No, definitely not | No, I don't think so | Yes, I think so | Yes, definitely |

WRITE COMMENTS BELOW

*Can be used as a shorter scale.

*Note:* From "Assessment of Client Patient Satisfaction: Development of a General Scale" by D. Larsen, C. Attkisson, W. Hargreaves, and T. Nguyen, 1979, *Evaluation and Program Planning, 2,* 197-207. Copyright 1979 by Pergamon Press. Used with permission.

*Marital Observation Checklist.* The Marital Observation Checklist (MOC; Christensen & Nies, 1980) is a 179-item revision of the Spouse Observation Checklist (SOC; Patterson, 1976). The instrument uses 25 SOC "we" items, 77 SOC "spouse" items, and 77 specially created reciprocal "I" items (i.e., reciprocal of "spouse complimented me on my appearance" would be "I complimented spouse on his/her appearance"). Both the SOC and MOC are comprised of behaviorally referenced questions that are to be answered retrospectively with regard to the past 24-hour period. However, in contrast to the 400-item SOC, the MOC requires considerably less time to complete. Previous research has indicated that both measures are reliable, valid, and highly versatile in the assessment of marital interaction. Moreover, due to the intensive self-monitoring needed to complete either instrument, positive changes in the couple's relationship are often noted in response to administering the measures. Both instruments are capable of producing P : D ratios (pleasing : displeasing), which may prove useful in the overall evaluation of marital therapy effectiveness.

*Primary Communications Inventory.* The Locke-Sabagh-Thomas (1956) Primary Communication Inventory (PCI) adapted by Navran (1967) is a 25-item self- and spouse-report questionnaire designed to assess communication patterns between marital partners. Further, the PCI taps both verbal and nonverbal forms of communication. Specific items address such issues as talking about pleasant/unpleasant events, sulking, voice tone, and facial expression. Navran (1967) and Yelsma (1984) have shown that the PCI correlates highly with the Marital Relationship Inventory, a global measure of marital adjustment. In fact, Navran, like others, argues that communication and marital satisfaction co-vary to the extent that one must have an effect upon the other. In addition, Yelsma (1984) reports that the PCI has good internal reliability for both satisfied and dissatisfied couples.

*Marital Interaction Coding System.* The Marital Interaction Coding System (MICS; Hops, Wills, Patterson, & Weiss, 1972) is the most widely used direct observational coding system for the analysis of couples' interactions. The original MICS had 28 scoring categories designed to "objectively record verbal and nonverbal behaviors that occur as marriage partners attempt to negotiate, in a laboratory setting, resolution of their marital problems" (Hops et al., 1972, p. 1). Recent modifications of the MICS have improved the applicability of this instrument in clinical settings. Namely, summary codes have been employed in which 10 or 12 categories have been shown to be reliably predictive of either distress or satisfaction in individuals and couples (see Resick, Welsh-Osga, Zitomer, Spiegel, Meidlinger, & Long, 1980; Welsh-Osga, Resick, & Zitomer, 1981). In addition,

Weider and Weiss (1980) have demonstrated that the MICS can be used to score audiotaped as well as videotaped interactions. Using the MICS in conjunction with unobtrusive, in-home audio-recorders (designed to record samples of communication at undisclosed, predetermined times) also provides excellent assessment information as well as measures of treatment generality.

*Couples Interaction Scoring System.* The Couples Interaction Scoring System (CISS; Gottman et al., 1977) is the only coding system that produces two independent codes for each unit of interaction. The CISS is comprised of 28 verbal codes ("content" codes) and three nonverbal codes ("affect" codes). However, in data analysis, eight summary "content" codes are typically used: problem information, mind reading, proposing a solution, communication talk, agreement, disagreement, summarizing other, and summarizing self. One of three nonverbal codes (i.e., positive, neutral, negative) also is scored for each interaction unit. Thus, there are a total of 24 possible codes. Although the CISS provides a comprehensive description of couples' interactions, it is impractical as a marital measure for most practicing therapists. Moreover, unlike the MICS, the CISS does not lend itself to scoring audiotaped interactions and therefore is used only with videotaped sequences.

*Verbal Problem Checklist.* The Verbal Problem Checklist (VPC; Thomas, 1977; Thomas, Walter, & O'Flaherty, 1974) assesses couples' communication on the basis of direct observation. The VPC includes 49 categories of verbal behavior (see Table 3.5), which are rated on a 4-point Likert scale. An additional rating of the categories on a 1-3 scale is used to identify the degree to which each category represents a problem area for the couple. Although this instrument is less rigorous and systematic than the other observational coding systems (i.e., MICS, CISS), it requires only a minimum amount of time to complete, provides useful assessment data, and represents a highly practical clinical measurement strategy.

# SUMMARY

This chapter provided an overview and general description of intake interviews and marital assessment strategies. Particular attention was paid to highlighting practical and realistic measures for use in direct-care settings. The process of conducting an intake interview with couples was presented as serving three primary functions: (a) development of the therapeutic relationship, (b) collection of assessment information, and (c)

Table 3.5. Response Categories for Verbal Problem Checklist

| | |
|---|---|
| 1. Overtalk | 26. Topic content avoidance |
| 2. Undertalk | 27. Other content avoidance |
| 3. Fast talk | 28. Topic content shifting |
| 4. Slow talk | 29. Other content shifting |
| 5. Loud talk | 30. Topic content persistence |
| 6. Quiet talk | 31. Other content persistence |
| 7. Sing-song speech | 32. Poor referent specification |
| 8. Monotone speech | 33. Temporal remoteness |
| 9. Rapid latency | 34. Detached utterance |
| 10. Slow latency | 35. Positive talk deficit |
| 11. Affective talk | 36. Positive talk surfeit |
| 12. Unaffective talk | 37. Acknowledgment deficit |
| 13. Obtrusions | 38. Acknowledgment surfeit |
| 14. Quibbling | 39. Opinion deficit |
| 15. Overresponsiveness | 40. Opinion surfeit |
| 16. Underresponsiveness | 41. Excessive agreement |
| 17. Excessive question asking | 42. Excessive disagreement |
| 18. Pedantry | 43. Dysfluent talk |
| 19. Dogmatic statement | 44. Too little information given |
| 20. Overgeneralization | 45. Redundant information given |
| 21. Undergeneralization | 46. Too much information given |
| 22. Excessive cueing | 47. Negative talk surfeit |
| 23. Incorrect autalitic | 48. Negative talk deficit |
| 24. Presumptive attribution | 49. Illogical talk |
| 25. Misrepresentation of fact or evaluation | |

*Note:* From *Marital Communication and Decision-Making* by E. J. Thomas, 1977, Copyright 1977 by The Free Press, a Division of Macmillan, Inc. Used with permission.

implementation of mutual therapeutic regimes. In addition, details of the intake procedure were described. Recommendations were offered regarding formal measurement strategies that may be employed. The role of self-, spouse-, and external-observer assessment of marital interaction was reviewed. The chapter concluded with an examination of specific assessment instruments.

# Chapter 4
# Therapeutic Tactics, Strategies and Procedures

In Chapter 2, we elaborated five principles of relationship change: (a) creating a positive working relationship, (b) understanding behavior, (c) objectification, (d) behavioral exchange, and (e) compromise. In the present chapter, we will attempt to demonstrate means by which these principles are actually put to practice by behavioral-communications marital therapists. Although space limitations do not permit us to detail all of the behavioral-communications techniques, a representative sampling will be provided. In later chapters we will deal with the separate topics of communications and problem-solving training. Further techniques will be elaborated at that time. The reader will note, however, that although the topics of communications and problem-solving training are removed from the present discussion, there is considerable overlap between them and the above five principles. This distinction is drawn primarily for didactic purposes.

## TECHNIQUES FOR CREATING A POSITIVE WORKING RELATIONSHIP

For organizational purposes, we will discuss techniques used in the development of a working relationship from three major perspectives: (a) interpersonal skills of the therapist, (b) tactical skills of the therapist, and (c) relationship between marital partners.

## Interpersonal Skills of the Therapist

The key interpersonal skills we previously discussed were self-confidence, "human-ness," and self-disclosure. Although the skills are, no doubt, highly correlated with one another, let us examine them independently.

MT-C

*Self-confidence.* There are unquestionably hundreds of discrete behaviors that imply self-confidence on the part of the therapist. These may range from a simple, yet firm handshake to explicit statements regarding one's professional abilities. Perhaps the display of self-confident behaviors has its greatest import during the intake interview sessions. As a consequence, we have a series of opening and closing remarks that we typically employ during the first session, in part, as a demonstration of therapist assurance and self-confidence.

### Opening Remarks

*Therapist:* My plan for today's session is as follows. First, I'd like to get to know you folks a little. Second, I'll need some information about what brings you in. Third, while I want to hear from you, I will be asking a considerable number of questions today. Finally, by the time we are finished, I'd like to be able to give you some initial feedback and let you know if I think I can be of service to you.
*Wife:* Okay, where would you like us to begin?
*Therapist:* (*looking at both partners*) Well, where would you like to begin?

The purpose of this strategy is actually fourfold. First, we want to demonstrate to the couple that the therapist is knowledgeable, experienced, and organized—in essence, that the therapist knows what he/she is doing; second, that a clear "game plan" exists both for this session and perhaps throughout the course of therapy; and third, that the therapist is "in charge" and can anticipate the sequence of events that might occur. Lastly, this strategy will demonstrate that although the therapist is somewhat structured in his/her approach to working with couples, there is enough flexibility to accommodate clients' personal idiosyncratic needs.

### Closing Remarks

*Therapist:* We only have a few minutes left, so I'd like to take our remaining time to give you a little feedback. You folks did an excellent job today. You provided me with lots of information and really did fill me in on your relationship both presently and in the past. Obviously, there are questions that yet remain, but we can deal with those in our upcoming assessment sessions. I am prepared at this time, however, to make the following comments. First, I do believe I can be of some service. Your relationship is quite similar to couples' situations that I frequently work with. Second, although this is only our first hour together, I am relatively optimistic about the likelihood of aiding you in changing your situation—and obviously, that's why you're here. Third, I will need one or two further assessment sessions with you in order to get a complete picture of your marriage. Finally, at the close of that assessment period I intend to let you know how I see things. At that time, we can then jointly decide where we go from there. Okay, do you have any questions for me?

The reader will note some obvious similarities between our opening and closing remarks. Namely, we once again intend to appear experienced, organized, and highly self-assured. In addition, we have complimented our clients on their efforts during the first session and informed them of the continuing assessment meetings that will be required. Further, where appropriate, we immediately acknowledge our optimism regarding the likelihood of change. Lastly, we close our comments by implying that all decisions are collaborative in nature. Thus, no one feels forced into treatment and instead chooses of his/her own free will.

Obviously, there are a number of other ways in which therapist self-confidence can be expressed both in the intake session and throughout the course of therapy. Although one does not want to appear boastful or egotistical, he/she does want to make it clear to clients that the therapist is the expert. In point of fact, we are the experts. For, if they knew more than we do, their relationship would not be in quite its present condition!

*"Human-ness."* In Chapter 2, we provided a short example of how clients often enter therapy with some rather strange ideas about their therapists. Presently, we would like to demonstrate techniques that one might use to allay these anxieties and further present oneself as a relatively normal human being. The two examples provided in the following accomplish this through the use of humor and nonjudgmental acceptance.

*Humor*

*Husband:* We always seem to be arguing; we just don't seem to be able to get along anymore.
*Wife:* That's it exactly! Either he's in a bad mood or I'm in a bad mood, but we never seem to be in the same place at the same time.
*Therapist:* Yeah, I noticed that you two even came in different doors of the clinic when you arrived today. (*smiling*)
*Husband:* (*laughing*) That's us all right. She says yes and I say no, I say yes and she says no.
*Therapist:* (*to husband*) I've got it! If you start saying yes all of the time, you guys will be in agreement on at least 50% of the occasions. And, some of those yesses may turn out to be a whole lot of fun!
*Husband/Wife:* (*both laughing*)

This simple example is provided as a means of demonstrating "human-ness" of the therapist. In this particular instance, humor was used to lighten the atmosphere and create a more workable situation. So long as the couple took their problems so seriously, they were unable to relax and enjoy themselves. Thus, in this brief vignette, the therapist's humor actually had multiple purposes. Indeed, humor may serve a variety of functions in psychotherapy.

*Nonjudgmental Acceptance*

*Wife:* We've hit a low point like this in our relationship before.
*Therapist:* When was that?
*Wife:* Well, about 6 years ago things were really bad. I just couldn't take it anymore so I picked up and left.
*Therapist: (to couple)* What was going on back then? I mean, what was happening in your lives that was so upsetting?
*Husband:* Quite honestly, it was the "shits." I was out of work and was a real bastard to live with. Janie tried her best to put up with me, but she could only take it for so long, and rightfully so. I didn't blame her at all for leaving. Don't get me wrong, I was upset when she left but I knew it was the right thing for her to do.
*Therapist:* Sounds like you really must have been down on yourself back then.
*Husband:* Yeah, I'm sure I was, but so was Janie—weren't you? *(to wife)*
*Wife:* You bet. I really felt like a quitter walking out on Fred like that. I knew I should stay and try to work things out but it just seemed hopeless. I didn't know what else to do.
*Therapist:* So you both were in a real difficult situation and tried your best not to lose it entirely. And you find yourselves in a somewhat similar situation right now, is that right?
*Husband:* Well, sort of. . . . (starts talking about present difficulty)

In this example, the therapist quite clearly communicates an empathic understanding of the clients' past and present difficulties. Moreover, this is done with concern, acceptance, and interpersonal support for both partners. By demonstrating this type of sensitivity, the couple is apt to feel safe, understood, and willing to work further with this therapist who undoubtedly is there to help, not hurt.

*Self-disclosure.* As indicated earlier, therapist self-disclosure can be a useful instrument in facilitating the process of change. Its employment in the following discussion best exemplifies this.

*Husband:* So I asked our son, Bill, if he wanted to help me build this bookcase that I had promised to do, but he said he was doing some things with his friends and was busy.
*Therapist:* How did you feel about that?
*Husband:* Okay, I guess. He's a teenager now and I know he's got his things to do. I can't expect him to want to hang around the house and just mess around with his dad.
*Therapist:* Boy, that sounds real similar to what I went through just a couple of years ago. All of a sudden my daughter was no longer a kid but more like a grown woman—her friends, her interests, her own thing. I felt pretty left out . . . and pretty hurt. It wasn't easy.
*Husband:* Yeah, sometimes I feel that way but it's to be expected, isn't it? Kids do have to grow up, don't they?
*Therapist:* I guess so, but right now I'm wondering if Sue *(wife)* even knows that Bill's growing up can be difficult for you.

*Husband:* I don't know, we never really talk about it like that.
*Therapist:* Maybe that's something you need to talk about.

In the previous example, therapist self-disclosure truly did open some doors. By providing an example from his own personal experience, the therapist aided the client in getting in touch with some of his previously denied feelings of isolation and pain. More importantly, the therapist then translated these feelings back into the relationship by informing the couple that they may want to talk about just these kinds of things. In point of fact, they went on to do this and really grew as a result of the experience. The wife was glad to know that her husband "felt" at all (she had formerly complained that he never shared or talked to her about his feelings), and he, in turn, found a new and willing co-worker in his wife. Therapist self-disclosures thus opened both behavioral and communications avenues that had previously been closed.

## Tactical Skills of the Therapist

In Chapter 2, we discussed four major tactical skills that we considered to be of prime importance: (a) control, (b) activity level, (c) language, and (d) building affective-behavioral bridges. We will now attempt to demonstrate their technical use and application within the context of the marital therapy session.

*Control.* There are so many different ways in which therapists take control in marital therapy that we simply cannot do service to the topic in this one small section. In fact, the reader should already be aware of positive therapeutic control examples as expressed in our intake and evaluation procedure (see Chapter 3). Further, control-related material will be provided in the communications, problem-solving, and extended case example chapters. Presently, however, we would like to provide two techniques for garnering control. The first is much broader and provides the reader with a general strategy for assuming control. In this example, our parenthetical comments are intended to demonstrate what it is that the therapist is thinking. As a consequence, we refer to it as the "internal dialogue technique." In the second technique, we will demonstrate the use of control within the physical setting of the therapy room.

### Internal Dialogue Techniques

*Sara:* I feel like our life is boring. We never have anything to talk about and when we do talk, we talk about nothing. You know, what's going to be on television this evening, how the Broncos are doing or some other junk like that. It's boring, just plain boring.
*Mike:* What are people supposed to talk about? That's what people talk

about. You remind me of Jack at my office. He comes in and gripes all day long—tells me how rotten the work is, how underpaid we are, how the boss is cleaning up and we can't make ends meet. That's bullshit. Work is work. I enjoy my work. It may not be the greatest job in the world, but I think I'm pretty good at what I do and a pretty good provider for my family.

*Therapist:* (*What's going on in here? Sara starts off talking about how they don't meaningfully communicate, and Mike defensively drifts off the topic. My guess is that Mike is quite threatened by this kind of conversation and really doesn't want to see it continue. Let's check that out.*) Sara, I'm wondering what happens when you bring this kind of conversation up at home?

*Sara:* Nothing, nothing happens at all. In fact, sometimes I wonder if he even hears me. But I know he hears me because sometimes he'll answer me and tell me, "You're crazy, we talk all the time, what's wrong with you anyhow?" If you call that something happening, then something happens. Personally, it seems to me like it's a waste of time to even bring it up. All it does is get both of us either angry or frustrated.

*Therapist:* (*Aha, I think I was right. Sara brings up their lack of meaningful conversation and Mike angrily flees. That's exactly what's happening in here right now. Well, what would I like to see happen instead? That's obvious. I'd like to see Sara get her point across more effectively without Mike having to feel attacked. Okay, that's good, but how am I going to accomplish that? I've got it. First, I'll try playing the role of Sara and making my comments in a much more reasonable tone. If that doesn't work, maybe I can get Mike to tell her that she really puts him off when she sounds so accusing. I'll give that a try and see what happens.*) Okay, I'd like to try something different here. Sara, I'd like to play your role for a minute and see if we can take this a little further. . . .

The key issue in the internal dialogue technique revolves around three major questions: (a) What's going on in here? (b) Where do I want to go? and (c) How do I get there? In raising and then answering these questions, the therapist not only takes control, but provides direction based on his/her working conceptualization. The technique is essential. In fact, we would venture to guess that it is the most significant of all behavioral-communications strategies that can be used within individual sessions because it is so widely employable. That is, the technique has applicability across a wide array of problem areas and different forms of couples' interaction.

*Control within the Physical Setting.* As part of our standard operating procedure, we always arrange the chairs in the therapy room prior to beginning the actual therapy session. As indicated in Figure 4.1, this arrangement is primarily dependent upon the number of therapists present. With one therapist in the room, the chairs are triangulated. That is, individuals may choose any chair in the triangle and still sit equidistant from one another. In addition, the chairs are turned so that they all face a midpoint, intersecting at the center of the triangle. There are a number of reasons

**With Couple and One Therapist**

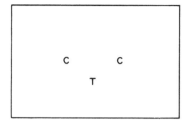

**With Couple and Two Therapists**

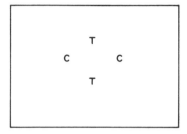

C = Client

T = Therapist

FIGURE 4.1. Physical Arrangement of Chairs in Therapy Room

for this arrangement. First, individuals are provided with the illusion of freedom, because they have a choice among chairs, but all choices result in the same triangular form. Second, equidistancing between chairs prevents uncontrolled alliances from forming. Although we have no problem with the formation of alliances, we want to be in control of such alliances if and when they occur. Third, by centering the chairs as we do, partners are provided with direct access to one another. As will soon become apparent, we consider the facilitation of direct communication to be one of the major building blocks of effective interaction between couples. When two therapists are present in the room, the situation changes slightly. Couples are not given the freedom to choose any chair they wish because therapists will initially want to sit directly across from one another. In so doing, they and the clients are, once again, afforded the opportunity of directly communicating with one another.

As an example of control in the physical setting, we are reminded of a situation that happened a few years ago. One of us had an initial appointment with a couple with whom we had never met. The chairs had been prearranged in accord with Figure 4.1 (with one therapist present). Upon entering the room, the husband immediately picked up one chair, moved it to a far corner, and promptly sat down, physically creating great distance between himself and the other two chairs (see Figure 4.2). With that, the therapist hesitated for a moment and then quickly moved his chair across the room, once again establishing the formation of an equilateral triangle. At that point the session then began. What became immediately evident was that the husband was extremely reluctant to participate. This was openly addressed, and under no circumstances was the therapist going to allow himself to become part of a wife-therapist collusive process. To have done so, at any level, only would have provided the hus-

Husband's Arrangement of Chairs

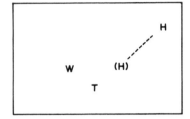

H = Husband's chair

W = Wife's chair

T = Therapist's chair

Therapist's Re-arrangement of Chairs

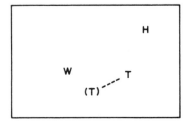

FIGURE 4.2. Arrangement of Chairs with Reluctant Husband

band with greater cause to never begin or prematurely leave therapy. Thus, we continue to believe that therapist control remains a cornerstone of effective therapy.

*Activity Level.* We have previously discussed therapist activity level from both a cognitive and behavioral perspective. Cognitively, one remains active in therapy by constantly raising and answering questions regarding the content and process of treatment. This is virtually identical to the "internal dialogue technique" just previously elaborated. Slight differences may occur with respect to the specific questions raised, but basically the same process is at play. That is, activity within the cognitive realm is a function of forcing oneself to maintain a mental alertness in therapy. Active therapists, then, are those who are constantly covertly questioning themselves and the actions of their clients in an effort to provide the most efficacious treatment.

Behavioral activity follows quite logically from cognitive activity. In essence, therapists make decisions regarding what type of intervention they might pursue. However, given the repetitive patterns of interaction that couples tend to exhibit, therapeutic action must be swift and provide for the generation of alternative behaviors on the part of the couple. Such is the case in the following example.

*Holly:* I want you to be more of a "man." I'd feel so much better about you if once in a while you would lead rather than follow. But, you never do. You always leave everything up to me. I feel like I make all of the decisions in this family and I'm tired of it.

*Jim:* I'd like to lead but . . . I don't know . . . that's not easy for me.

*Therapist:* Hold on. Jim, let me see if I can help you out for a moment. (*Therapist pulls chair over next to Jim and whispers in his ear, "Using your own words, why don't you try telling Holly that you don't make decisions as quickly as she does. If you're going to begin making some of these decisions, she's going to have to back off some and give you a little more time to decide what you want to do. What do you think?" Therapist remains in chair seated next to Jim.*)

*Jim:* Okay. Well, you know, if you gave me more time to make some of these decisions, I think I could do it. Like, calling about the home heating oil. I was going to do that and, before I even had a chance, you went and spoke to the man and the next thing I knew we had bought 500 gallons of oil. If you had given me a little more time, I would have been happy to take care of it.

*Therapist:* (*still whispering in Jim's ear, "In fact, I would have liked to take care of it."*)

*Jim:* Yeah, I would have enjoyed doing that. Now, in all honesty, there are some things that I wouldn't enjoy doing, but that's certainly not one of them.

*Therapist:* (*pulling chair back to original position; therapist now turns to wife and says, "That kind of puts you in a tough spot. First, how are you supposed to know which decisions he wants to make and which decisions he doesn't want to make? Second, just how long do you have to wait for him to make a decision? Some decisions need to be made pretty quick, don't they? Maybe you'd better check that out with him—let's do that one at a time. First, which decisions does he want to make?"*)

*Holly:* All right, what kinds of things do you want to make decisions about?

From this point onward, Jim and Holly began specifying the parameters of his decision-making. For our present purposes, however, there are a number of other elements worthy of comment. First, the therapist used the active technique of whispering. By pulling his chair over next to Jim and then whispering suggestions in his ear, he clearly forms an alliance with the husband. More importantly, though, he provides movement within the therapeutic process. Jim now has a response, and he clearly has the therapist's permission to voice this response. Moreover, Holly (having seen the therapist whisper in her husband's ear) is less apt to challenge Jim's comments when they are actually aired. Second, by physically moving about the room and whispering in Jim's ear, Jim's comments, undoubtedly, have greater impact and salience within the therapy hour. Lastly, after having made his point, the therapist returns his chair and forms an alliance with Holly. In so doing, he demonstrates an ability to align himself with both partners, thereby alienating neither. Indeed, the previous excerpt demonstrates both forms of activity—cognitive and behavioral. The behavioral activity is clearly overt, but based upon a well-conceived, covert, cognitive plan of action.

*Language.* A number of language issues have already been addressed. The following excerpt provides a very simple example of how therapist language can be used to cut through the vague words that sometimes impede the flow of therapy.

*LeAnn:* You never hold me, you never kiss me except when you want some sex, you never tell me that I look nice, you never even say nice things to me.

*Hal:* I tell you that you look nice. Just today before we came over here I asked you if that was a new dress because I didn't think I had seen it before.

*LeAnn:* So you asked me if it was a new dress. Is that supposed to mean you think I look pretty in it? Am I supposed to take that as a compliment?

*Hal:* I don't know what you're supposed to take it as. I don't understand you at all.

*Therapist:* Of course not. You're missing the point, Hal! What she's saying is, "Do you *really* care about me?"

*Husband:* (*silence*)

*Wife:* (*weepy*)

*Therapist:* (*to husband*) Well, do you?

*Husband:* (*softly*) Of course I do.

*Therapist:* Then you'd better find a way to show her!

Here, the reader will want to notice the crisp, clear, almost poignant phrasing used by the therapist. Moreover, the verbal interventions virtually demand a response from the husband. As indicated earlier, such comments are quite powerful and appear to have a directed therapeutic purpose in mind.

*Building Affective-behavioral Bridges.* Integrating affect and behavior is a means by which therapists provide clients with alternative ways of understanding their partner's feelings and actions. In so doing, the effective therapist opens avenues for exploration and possible change.

> *Ann:* You know, you have your thing and I have mine, but we never seem to do anything together.
> *George:* I know, and I'm not sure why. We used to do lots of things together, but that really doesn't happen very much anymore.
> *Ann:* Yes, but you don't seem bothered by that. I know that's real upsetting to me, but you seem to accept it as just the way things are, and there's nothing we can do about it.
> *George:* Well, I guess that's sort of right. I think it happens because we're both so busy—what with our schedules as they are and, at least for the foreseeable future, things don't look like they're going to change very much.
> *Ann:* Uh, huh. I think we've got a real problem here. I'm upset about this, and I find myself getting more and more upset. You just keep rolling along accepting the status quo, and I'll tell you, it's unacceptable to me.
> *Therapist:* Ann, I get the impression that you think George isn't the least bit bothered by your lack of time together. I guess I've heard him say in the past that doing things together was something that he valued—something that he felt real good about.
> *Ann:* (*to George*) Is that true?
> *George:* Absolutely, but I'm not sure what we can do about our present situation. We're really tied into things.
> *Therapist:* (*to George*) And that's real frustrating to you.
> *George:* You bet! (*to Ann*) I don't like it anymore than you do. I want us to have more time together, but right now it seems almost impossible.
> *Ann:* Well, I think we just can't give up—we have to find a way. But I have to admit, it's nice to know that you're upset about it, too.
> *George:* Believe me, I am.
> *Therapist:* Okay, now what can you two do about it to improve the situation a little?

In the previous example, Ann had misunderstood George's behavior. She assumed that because he was not complaining, he must be satisfied with the present situation. The therapist, however, did not believe that to be the case. As a consequence, he attempted to point out the difference between George's feelings and George's behavior. Once this was accomplished, Ann clearly recognized that she and George were not quite so far apart on this issue. Ann felt a lot better, and George finally got to talk some about his frustration. They then went on to try to behaviorally improve the situation just a bit.

## Building a Working Relationship
## Between Partners

As we indicated in Chapter 2, building a positive working relationship between partners is an essential but not necessarily simple task. We have already indicated a variety of generic ways in which this may be accomplished. Two very basic tactics that we frequently employ are the "history of the romance" procedure and the "tell me what you like" technique.

*"History of the Romance" Technique.* Frequently, couples will enter therapy fully prepared to cite one complaint after another. Certainly, the therapist must be willing to listen to some of this, otherwise the client feels that he/she has not been heard. However, there comes a point when a continued listing of grievances only does further damage to the marital relationship. In the example below, the therapist clearly felt that point had been reached. As a consequence, the "history of the romance" technique was employed.

> *Therapist:* I think I've got a pretty good idea of some of your present difficulties and certainly we'll get back to them, but right now I'd like to go in a slightly different direction. You folks haven't really filled me in on your early years together. For example, how did you meet?
> *Terry:* We met at college. Barb was sort of friendly with another girl I was dating. We got to know each other then, and eventually we started going out.
> *Therapist: (smiling and looking at Barb)* Oh, you mean you stole him away from your friend?
> *Barb:* Well, not exactly. *(slight laugh)* That relationship with the friend wasn't really going anyplace, and eventually they just kind of drifted apart. Terry ended up calling me, I asked the friend if she minded, she didn't, and so we started going out together.
> *Therapist: (to Terry)* What made you call her in the first place? I mean, what was it that attracted you to Barb?
> *Terry:* I was attracted to her right from the start, even when I was still dating Jill, her girlfriend.
> *Barb:* You were? You never told me that.
> *Terry:* Didn't I? I thought I did. In fact, we sort of went out one time before Jill and I even broke up.
> *Barb:* I don't remember that.
> *Terry:* Sure you do. Remember, we happened to meet at the laundromat one night. We were both doing our wash, and we went across the street and had some ice cream together during the "rinse and spin" cycle. *(both laugh)*

*Barb:* Well, that wasn't exactly a date!

*Terry:* Maybe it wasn't a date, but I sure had visions of "making it" with you even then. *(big smile)*

*Barb:* *(sarcastically)* Things haven't changed.

*Therapist:* Well, once you actually started dating, how long did you go together before you married?

*Barb:* Actually, quite some time. About two years.

*Therapist:* Uh, huh. And, what kinds of things did you used to do together back then?

*Barb:* Lots of fun things—we danced, bowled, went to the movies . . .

*Terry:* We did lots of athletic things together, too. Remember the co-rec volleyball team we were on?

*Barb:* Oh, my God, I'd totally forgotten about that! I was a terrible volleyball player.

*Terry:* No, you weren't, although I don't think I'll ever forget the time you nearly broke your arm when you got it caught in the net. Remember that? *(laughing)*

*Terry/Barb:* *(both laughing uncontrollably)*

In short, our experience with the "history of the relationship" technique is that it invariably brings forth positive memories when skillfully applied. Moreover, those positive memories can then be used to germinate a successful working relationship in the present. Obviously, the previous example is intended to give the reader a sense of how this might be accomplished. There is a wealth of questions that alternatively can be used. The reader is referred to Chapter 2 for further elaboration in this area.

*"Tell Me What You Like" Technique.* This is a second major technique that is used in an attempt to build a collaborative relationship between partners. In addition to serving as impetus for partners' cooperation, the technique also provides smooth transition for a variety of behavioral exchange procedures. Typically, the technique is employed either during initial assessment sessions or as homework between the close of the assessment period and the initiation of treatment. In either case, the procedure is most frequently used quite early in therapy. This makes good sense, because "early therapy" is the critical period for the development of a positive working relationship between partners. The assignment is usually given in the following manner:

*Therapist:* I have a homework assignment for you that I would like you to complete before our next session. You are to complete this assignment independently; that is, without showing it to your partner. The assignment is that I would like each of you to take a blank sheet of paper and label it "What I Like About My Partner." I then want you to write down any and all things you can think of about your spouse *that you appreciate.* The items can be as simple as "I like the fact that you're always well-dressed" or even something like "I like the way that you cuddle with me in bed on cold, wintry nights." Simply number them and write them down on the piece of paper, starting at the top and working your way down. Don't worry about the actual number you end up with. We're not doing any comparisons between the number you each generate. However, when you come back in next week, be prepared to turn your sheets in to me and to share the information with your partner at that time. Okay, do you have any questions?

*June:* What if he can't come up with any? (*sarcastically*)

*Therapist:* Right now I'd like you, June, to take care of your business and you, Paul, to take care of yours. Don't worry about each other's lists, just do what's expected of you. Understand?

*Paul:* Sounds fine to me.

*Therapist:* June?

*June:* Sure—this should be very interesting!

Upon returning the following week, the therapist has a considerable amount of work to accomplish. First, of course, is to use the technique to facilitate positive, cooperative behavior between partners. Second, by using the "tell me what you like" lists, the therapist actually begins the process of operationalization and behavioral specification. Third, as indicated earlier, the lists serve as a first-order approximation of behavioral exchange. More along these lines will be presented shortly.

## UNDERSTANDING BEHAVIOR

It has been stated that the meaning of any behavior is the response it elicits, regardless of the intent of the communicator (Bandler, Grinder, & Satir, 1976). Although we generally agree with this notion, we also believe that some behavior is simply behavior, and some behavior is a statement about the relationship. Frequently, direct interventions will bring about immediate and dramatic change with respect to some problem behavior. On other occasions, however, direct interventions may repeatedly fail. It is at this point that the therapist must consider the behavior in its relational context. That is, when partners' reasonable requests for behavior change simply do not produce the desired results, one must question the function of the behavior. Does the behavior serve some purpose both for the individual and in the relationship?

### Changing Behavior as Behavior

*Ken:* You know, we've talked some about the different things that we both do that are somewhat upsetting to the other person. But we really haven't discussed the topic of sex. Maybe now that we're communicating a little bit better, we could take a look at that area as well.

*Therapist:* What did you have in mind?

*Ken:* Well, I think there are some things that could be a little bit better in that area and I'd be willing to talk about it if you were. (*to wife*)

*Sue:* Sure. What were you thinking of?

*Ken:* Well, I guess primarily that I always initiate sex. It's almost like if I don't start it, it doesn't happen. And, I guess I don't understand that.

*Sue:* You're right, you're definitely right. I don't understand it exactly either, but I know that's the way it is. I've noticed that, too.

*Ken:* Why is it that way? It doesn't have to be that way, does it?

*Sue:* I don't know why. I just know that it's real difficult for me to just sort of "come on" to you. I guess I expect that's the kind of thing a man should do to a woman—not the other way 'round.

*Therapist:* But if I hear you right, Ken, what you're saying is that once in a while, in fact, you'd like Sue to "come on" to you. Is that right?

*Ken:* Yeah, that's exactly right. I don't like always having to be the one responsible for initiating sex. I'd like it to be a bit more shared.

*Sue:* I agree. I think you're right. It's just that that's kind of hard for me.

*Therapist:* (*to Sue*) Is there anything that Ken can do that would make it a little easier for you?

*Sue:* Hmm, I think so. (*to Ken*) I think if you weren't so quick to rush into sex and were willing to just hug and kiss and hold me a little more, it would be easier, but I'm not sure.

*Therapist:* That's good information. Well, what do you say we give this a try over the next two weeks? Ken, you slow down and maybe give the lovemaking a little more time, and you, Sue, see if you might want to try initiating sex a little bit more. What do you think? Are you willing to give that a try?

*Ken:* I think it's a real good idea.

*Sue:* I'm willing. I think it's something that we both need to work on. It's a pattern that we've gotten into and maybe one that we do need to change.

The previous dialogue is a condensation of actual therapy exchange. What appears to have taken only a few minutes in transcript required almost 30 minutes to complete in reality. There are a number of points that should be noted. First, therapist interventions were clearly directed at keeping the couple on task, aiding them in reaching a solution to the problem. Second, the therapist once again translated the behavior into the relationship by asking Sue if there was anything Ken could do to make it easier for her. Third, because noncontingent change was called for on the part of both spouses, no one felt they were entirely to blame, and no one partner's behavior change was made contingent on the other's. Fourth, the couple was not pushed or forced to initiate a large-scale behavior change program. Rather, every effort was made to play down the amount of change being requested. As a consequence, the therapist used terms like "*maybe* give the lovemaking a *little more* time" and "see if you *might* want to *try* initiating sex a *little bit more.*" Had either individual felt coerced into change, we doubt very much whether the program would have been successful. Indeed, Ken and Sue were seen 2 weeks later, and the results were very positive. Sue had initiated sex on three separate occasions. Ken had increased the length of lovemaking, and both partners were pleased with themselves and each other. In this instance, tactfully dealing directly with the behavior was all that was required. Certainly, it may be that the behaviors served some function within the relationship and that function was obviated by virtue of the therapeutic intervention. However, the law of parsimony prevails. That is, when one can directly intervene to create change, by all means, do so. Unfortunately, that is not always the case.

### Changing Behavior Within Its Relational Context

*Therapist:* Jeanine, I get the impression that you're upset about something.
*Jeanine:* Yeah, I am. I'm upset with Rob.
*Therapist:* Uh, huh.
*Rob:* She's mad because I went out drinking with my friends on Friday night and didn't get home 'til four o'clock in the morning. That's what this is about.
*Therapist: (to Jeanine)* Is that right?
*Jeanine:* Not quite. I'm mad about the four in the morning, I'm mad because he called at six o'clock and said he was going for a drink, then called again at ten o'clock and said he'd be home later. I'm mad 'cause I had fixed dinner, I didn't know what was going on, I was worried, I was sitting there all by myself, and this kind of thing always happens—I'm tired of it.
*Rob: (smiling)* What can I say? I already apologized. I went out with the guys for a little drink after work. *(to therapist)* You know, one thing leads to another. You're having a good time; I probably had a little too much to drink, I'll admit that. *(to Jeanine)* I called home at ten o'clock, didn't I, to tell you I wouldn't be there? I said don't wait up for me—we were going over to Larry's to play cards.
*Jeanine:* Oh, and that's supposed to excuse you that you called me at ten o'clock? That doesn't excuse anything, that just shows how guilty you feel about being a drunk!
*Therapist:* Okay, hold it. *(As a result of previous sessions, the therapist knows a number of things about this couple: (a) if an intervention is not made, these cross-accusations will continue ad infinitum; (b) Rob acts without regard to Jeanine because he is afraid that she might control him; (c) Jeanine feels constantly taken advantage of and treated inequitably by Rob.)* Jeanine, obviously you're upset. But, like you said, it isn't just this one incident. You're upset because this kind of thing has repeatedly happened, and you really don't think it's fair.
*Jeanine:* That's right. I don't deserve this. I really don't. I deserve something better.
*Therapist:* And, Rob, I guess I've heard you say something similar. I've heard you say you don't deserve this either, but in a different kind of way. You don't deserve being treated like a child—always being told what to do. That's what really gets to you, isn't it?
*Rob:* It sure is. I'm 25 years old. I know what I'm doing. I don't need anyone telling me what, where, or how to do it!
*Therapist:* Those are the issues. The issue really isn't calling if you're going to be late or coming home at four in the morning. Certainly, it would help, Jeanine, if you knew what was going on and if you, Rob, could go

out for a little drink with the guys. But, the real issue for you, Jeanine, is being treated more fairly and for you, Rob, not being told what to do. Now, if you guys want to talk about that we might be able to accomplish something. But if you just want to sit here and lash out at each other, you're wasting both my time and yours.

*Jeanine:* Okay, how do we do that?

*Rob:* I'm willing, but I'm not sure what we do next either.

*Therapist:* Okay, let's take it one step at a time. Rob, you don't like it when Jeanine sometimes tells you what to do and treats you like a child. Without getting accusing, can you simply explain to her what that feels like for you?

*Rob:* I think so. . . .

This was a very difficult situation. The therapist was working with a rather explosive couple. Both Jeanine and Rob were already pretty angry, and it would not have taken much to distance them even further. Understanding the function of the clients's behavior, though, allowed the therapist to deal with the hidden agendas rather than a series of "brush fires." By not allowing the cross-complaining to continue, the therapist managed to *reframe* the clients' accusations in a somewhat more positive manner. It is interesting to note that, with this rather aggressive couple, the therapist had to intervene in an aggressive manner to get their attention. However, it worked. In addition, at the close of the transcript, the therapist purposely chose to first deal with Rob's issue rather than Jeanine's. It was reasoned that, had the converse occurred, Rob may have defensively sabotaged any of Jeanine's requests for change. Jeanine, on the other hand, was more apt to successfully make the changes desired by Rob. Once that occurred, there was an increased likelihood that Rob, too, would begin meeting some of the needs of his wife. In any case, it is incumbent upon the therapist to inform partners that both issues will be confronted, although we choose to do so one at a time.

## OBJECTIFICATION

As a result of the examples presented earlier, the reader should already have considerable familiarity with the principle of objectification. As a consequence, we will provide a relatively brief example of how objectification might actually be accomplished during the course of therapy.

When discussing building a positive relationship between partners we previously employed the "tell me what you like" technique. June and Paul were sent home to generate independent lists of things that they appreciated about their spouse. Table 4.1 is a copy of the homework assignment as originally completed by both partners. As is to be expected, a number of the comments are extremely vague and poorly defined. For ex-

Table 4.1. Homework Assignment: "Tell Me What You Like" Technique

| Things That I Appreciate About Paul | Things That I Appreciate About June |
|---|---|
| 1. Loyal | 1. Willingness to let me do my own things |
| 2. Active—likes to go places | 2. Supportive of my career decisions |
| 3. Talks about me nicely to others | 3. Generous of her time and energy |
| 4. Feels strongly about caring for his children | 4. Strong moral character and high ethical standards |
| 5. Honest | 5. Willing to stand up for and defend her beliefs |
| 6. Willing to help around the house | 6. Sincere |
| 7. Speaks his mind | 7. Strong sense of friendship |
| 8. Bright | 8. Compatible social and environmental beliefs to my own |
| 9. Considerate of others | |

ample, June noted that Paul was "loyal" and "speaks his mind." During the ensuing discussion, the therapist aided June in behaviorally specifying these positive characteristics. As might be expected, these were June's short-hand descriptors. "Loyal" actually meant "I know that you're trustworthy; you would never say anything nasty about me to some of your friends." Moreover, June was able to give Paul explicit examples of instances where he had been supportive of her in just this manner. Similarly, "speaks his mind" was further defined as, "I always know where you stand on matters; you're right up-front with your views on things, and that's something that I really appreciate." Once again, she was able to cite numerous examples of Paul's forthrightness. Paul's listing of June's positive attributes was also vague. "Willingness to let me do my own thing" actually translated into "I appreciate the fact that you're not jealous of the time I devote to my photography." "Strong sense of friendship" actually meant that "you really give of yourself to others without expecting anything in return—it's really admirable and something that I've always respected in you." Paul was very laudatory in this particular attribute and was able to give examples from both the recent and distant past. In all instances, the specification provided was initially at the prompting of the therapist. Short, yet vital questions served as the impetus for the provision of this information. Questions such as:

- "What does Paul do that demonstrates his loyalty to you?"
- "What is it about Paul's speaking his mind that you really appreciate?"
- "What leads you to believe that June is willing to let you do your own thing?"
- "How is it that June shows you a strong sense of friendship?"

Obviously, there is a multitude of questions, all of which may potentially increase informational specification between partners. It must be remembered that such specification is essential for both positive and negative behaviors, for, without explicit information, partners simply remain ignorant with regard to the means by which they can please or displease their mate. Ignorance may be bliss, but it certainly does not aid a marital relationship.

## BEHAVIORAL EXCHANGE

Although a variety of behavioral exchange techniques exists in the marital literature, presently we will focus on a variation of the "caring days" procedure (Stuart, 1980). The reader will note, however, that other behavioral exchange tactics are illustrated in the communications, problem-solving, and extended case example chapters (Chapters 5, 6, and 8).

The caring days technique is a means by which therapists provide distressed couples with an opportunity to reverse the downward spiral of their relationship. Rather than focusing on the negative, destructive forms of interaction, caring days provides couples with the opportunity to enter the reinforcing world of relationships. The instructions are very basic: "Make a list of the things your partner could do that would, once again, demonstrate that he/she really cared about you." After having obtained the listing, therapist and clients begin the task of behavioral specification. All items in the listing must be positive (e.g., "Kiss me at least once per day" is acceptable; "Don't ignore me" is unacceptable), well-specified, of a relatively high frequency (i.e., capable of being emitted daily), and not the subject of recent conflict. Once the listing has been refined in accordance with these requirements, spouses are then asked to make a caring days commitment. This commitment involves the simple statement: "I will do my best to carry out some of the caring days requests you've made, and I will try to do these on a daily basis." Further, partners are informed that *this is not a quid pro quo contract.* That is, they are responsible for carrying out as many of the behaviors on their partner's list as they can, regardless of what their partner has done for them. It is not a "something for something" arrangement. Obviously, should vast inequities occur, this will be grist for the therapeutic mill and undoubtedly prompt (under the therapist's guidance) a re-examination of the caring days commitment. Figure 4.3 provides an example of a caring days listing as prepared by both husband and wife. These lists were separately posted in the house, and spouses were asked to record behaviors at the close of each day. Before indicating that a behavior has occurred, individuals were to receive verification from their partner. Thus, from session to session, the therapist has a very clear idea as to the type and frequency of positive interactional behaviors.

FIGURE 4.3. Caring Days Lists for David and Ruth

| David's List | Date | | | | | | |
|---|---|---|---|---|---|---|---|
| Give me a backrub | 6/13 | | 6/15 | | | | 6/19 |
| Feed the dog | | 6/14 | | | 6/17 | 6/18 | |
| Kiss me | 6/13 | 6/14 | | 6/16 | | 6/18 | |
| Take me out for dinner | | | 6/15 | | | | |
| Call me at work | | 6/14 | | | 6/17 | | |
| Have sex with me | | 6/14 | | | | 6/18 | |
| Play racquetball with me | | | | 6/16 | | | |
| Go to bed when I do | 6/13 | 6/14 | | | 6/17 | 6/18 | |
| | | | | | | | |

| Ruth's List | Date | | | | | | |
|---|---|---|---|---|---|---|---|
| Tell me that I look nice | 6/13 | | 6/15 | | | | 6/19 |
| Fix lunch for both of us | | 6/14 | | | 6/17 | | |
| Put the cap on the toothpaste | 6/13 | 6/14 | 6/15 | 6/16 | 6/17 | 6/18 | 6/19 |
| Tell me about your day | 6/13 | 6/14 | | | | 6/18 | |
| Ask me about my day | 6/13 | 6/14 | | | | 6/18 | |
| Take me to the movies | | 6/14 | 6/15 | | | | |
| Look at me when you talk to me | 6/13 | 6/14 | | | 6/17 | | 6/19 |
| Sit next to me when we watch TV | | | 6/15 | 6/16 | | | |
| Go jogging with me | | | 6/15 | | | | |

A final note about the caring days procedure. Although we tend to use the technique to increase positive forms of relating, it can certainly be appropriately used later in therapy to decrease negative interactions. In either case, we have found it to be a highly reactive self-monitoring tool, because it clearly influences the behavior in question (Bornstein, Hamilton, & Bornstein, 1985). Moreover, in the vast majority of instances, this reactivity is congruent with the valence of the behavior (i.e., positive behaviors increase, and negative behaviors decrease). When this occurs, couples find a change in their overall evaluation of the relationship. That is, they truly begin caring about and enjoying each other once again.

## COMPROMISE

In this closing section of the chapter, we can perhaps best demonstrate how therapeutic compromise can be achieved by examining the transcript of a couple in therapy.

*Norma:* I know that we rescheduled to spend Christmas at your mother's house this year, but I think we've got to change our plans.

*Wally:* What do you mean?

*Norma:* Well, my mother's been sick and this may be her last Christmas. I doubt very much that she's going to live to see the Christmas after this one. Christmas means a lot to her, and I think she would really be thrilled to have us and all of her grandchildren together on this one last family occasion.

*Wally:* I know she's sick, but she ain't died yet! What if she keeps lingering on like this? Does that mean we have to spend every Christmas until she does die at your folks' house? That doesn't sound very fair to me.

*Norma:* Well, I don't think that's going to happen. The doctor said she's failing—that her heart just isn't strong enough to support her. I guess, if by some miracle, she did start to get better, then we could go back to our original plan of switching Christmas every other year.

*Wally:* I don't like it. We're scheduled to go to my parents' house and that's the way I think it should stay.

*Therapist:* (*at this point it's become clear that Norma and Wally are "stuck"; consequently, therapeutic intervention is required if any movement is to occur.*) Are those the only two alternatives, going to Norma's folks' house or going to Wally's folks?

*Wally:* What do you mean? Who else's home would we go to?

*Therapist:* I don't know, but you two are making it sound like either you go to one place or you go to the other . . . as if there are no other options.

*Norma:* Well, there aren't really.

*Therapist:* Really?

*Norma:* I'm getting confused. If we don't go to my mother's house, then, of course, we'll go to Wally's. And, if we don't go to Wally's folks' house, then we're sure to go to mine. That's it.

*Therapist:* All I'm asking is, "Is that really it?" Have you explored all the options?

*Wally:* Huh, maybe not. I guess we could go to neither one.
*Norma:* That doesn't solve anything, but maybe we could manage to split it some way.
*Therapist:* Now you're thinking.
*Norma:* Yeah, maybe we could go to your mom's for Christmas eve and Christmas morning, and then go over to my folks' place for Christmas day—I don't know, something like that might work. It wouldn't be perfect, but I certainly think it would be better than our present plans.
*Wally:* That's an interesting idea. I might be willing to go for it, but I guess I'd like to think about it a little more . . . gee, it sure would make it a whole lot easier if your mom would just croak before Christmas! (*laughing*)
*Norma:* You know, you're a very sick person. (*smiling*)
*Wally:* I know that. Why do you think I'm here in the first place? (*smiling*)

The previous transcript is self-explanatory. The therapist gave the couple the opportunity to solve the problem by themselves and they could not do it. Simple questioning then led to the exploration of new alternatives, one of which seemed quite reasonable. Their proposed solution and light-hearted banter all indicate that they were pleased with their own work. Indeed, compromise appears to have carried the day.

## SUMMARY

This chapter was directly related to the material presented in Chapter 2 (Principles of Relationship Change). However, in the present chapter, attempts were made to demonstrate explicit techniques used in the practice of marital therapy. Consequently, a variety of therapeutic procedures were illustrated in the areas of: (a) creating a positive working relationship, (b) understanding behavior, (c) objectification, (d) behavioral exchange, and (e) compromise. The interested reader is referred back to each of the topical areas for specific tactical suggestions.

# Chapter 5
# Increasing Couples' Communications

## "WE'VE GOT A COMMUNICATIONS PROBLEM"

How frequently do clinicians hear this complaint? Estimates indicate that as many as 90% of all distressed couples cite communications difficulties as a major problem in their relationships. Unfortunately, the term is so generic that it rarely provides the practitioner with any meaningful information. In Chapter 1 we indicated that behavioral research supports the notion that communications problems mark the relationships of distressed couples. Now let us examine that more closely.

To begin, it is essential that we define the topic of this chapter. By *communication*, we refer to all symbolic means by which individuals transmit messages. This is most commonly accomplished via the use of words and extended verbal behavior. However, nonverbal behavior serves as yet another large category of communication. Included here would be such things as voice tone, body language, posture, appearance, facial cues, and so on. Regardless of the communication form or content, the symbols employed must be mutually shared if the message is to be adequately understood. Quite simply, if meaning is not shared, miscommunication is bound to occur. Thus, the generic term *communications problem* refers to the inadequate transmission of symbolic messages. In practical terms, it appears as though communications deficits are central to the occurrence of marital distress. How and what people talk about will influence their level of satisfaction in a relationship. Given the above, it is not surprising that most marital practitioners agree that communications training should be a part of virtually all couple-based treatment programs.

# COMBINING SCIENCE AND PRACTICE

Imagine the following scenario:

> Greg comes into the house, sneaks up behind his wife, Joyce, and begins
> tickling and affectionately wrestling with her. Joyce screams, "Stop, please
> stop," but Greg continues playfully jousting her about until she is finally
> able to set herself free. She gets up from the floor and angrily snaps at him,
> "What's the matter with you? Didn't you hear me ask you to stop? I don't
> like that kind of stuff." Greg is shocked and simply responds by saying, "I
> was playing; just trying to have some fun. I didn't mean any harm." They
> both go their separate ways bothered by what has just happened and con-
> fused by their partner's apparent insensitivity.

What we have witnessed is a classic example of differential relational
currencies (Villard & Whipple, 1976). In essence, what constitutes a caring message for one person may be interpreted as rejection by someone
else. Indeed, the message is a function of individual perceptions. When
people communicate in a manner that provides meaning about affection
or caring dimensions of a relationship, it is referred to as relational currency. There are two major forms of such currencies: intimate and economic. Intimate currency has to do with the personal verbal and nonverbal ways of sending relationship messages. Smiles, winks, hugs, and
playful wrestling may all be ways of expressing affection. The act itself is a
statement: "I wrestle with you on the floor because I really like you." For
most nondistressed couples, the intent of the message is quite clear. As
indicated earlier, however, distressed couples frequently experience wide
discrepancies between communicational intent and communicational impact (Gottman, Notarius, Markman et al., 1976). The intent–impact dis-
crepancy is probably even greater with respect to economic currencies.
This may involve the giving of material possessions, doing favors, or sharing something with another person. Here the avenues of interpretation
are even broader. Going out for a candlelight dinner may mean "I love
you." However, it may also be interpreted as reparation for a recent, undisclosed act of indiscretion. Because economic currency messages tend
not to be as clear, there is greater room for misperception and interpersonal misunderstanding. We believe there is a significant point to be made
here; that is, research in the area of marital conflict, satisfaction, communication, and decision-making has made tremendous strides over the
past decade. Marital researchers have learned quite a bit about couples'
relationships and what actually characterizes effective intimate interaction.
What must now be accomplished, however, is a translation of that knowl-
edge into efficacious treatment programs for the remediation and preven-

tion of marital distress. The communications training program described in this chapter is directed toward just that goal.

## A SAMPLING OF COMMUNICATIONS DIFFERENCES BETWEEN DISTRESSED AND NONDISTRESSED COUPLES

A host of laboratory-based investigations has been employed as a means of studying the manner in which distressed and nondistressed couples actually interact and communicate. We would like to briefly review the major applied findings derived from this body of research as follows.

1. Distressed and nondistressed couples do not differ with respect to the *intention* of their communications; however, distressed spouses do *perceive* their partner's remarks as significantly less positive than do nondistressed spouses (Gottman, Notarius, Markman et al., 1976).

2. In general, during conflict resolution tasks, distressed couples engage in significantly more negative behaviors than do nondistressed couples. Conversely, positive behaviors are more common in the repertoires of nondistressed couples. No major differences occur during casual conversation (Birchler et al., 1975; Vincent et al., 1975, 1979).

3. Distressed couples exhibit a lesser agreement to disagreement ratio than nondistressed couples (Gottman et al., 1977; Riskin & Faunce, 1972).

4. Nonverbal behavior is a powerful discriminator between distressed and nondistressed couples (Kahn, 1970). As would be expected, distressed couples exhibit significantly more negative nonverbal behavior than nondistressed couples (Gottman et al., 1977).

5. Distressed couples exhibit a greater likelihood of negative reciprocity than nondistressed couples (Gottman et al., 1977). More importantly, though, in terms of discrimination, displeasing spousal behavior is the most useful predictor of daily satisfaction ratings for distressed couples. Conversely, pleasing spousal behavior is the most useful predictor of daily satisfaction for nondistressed couples (Jacobson et al., 1980).

6. During conflict resolution tasks, distressed couples tend to engage in more "summarizing-self" and cross-complaining than "summarizing-other" sequences. This suggests poor listening and partner validation skills (Gottman et al., 1977).

7. Related to the previous items, a variety of other molecular behaviors (e.g., complaints, criticisms, volume, sarcasm, etc.) have been found to differentiate distressed from nondistressed couples engaged in problem-

solving communication (e.g., Klier & Rothberg, 1977; Resick, Sweet, Kieffer, Barr, & Ruby, 1977).

8. A variety of positive communication styles such as empathic, appropriate expression of feeling, "perceptual competence" (understanding one's partner) and so on appear highly correlated with marital satisfaction (Davidson, Balswick, & Halverson, 1983; Ely, Guerney, & Stover, 1973; Gottman & Porterfield, 1981).

9. Interpersonal trust, level of regard, and expression of affection have been repeatedly found to be positively associated with marital quality (Cousins & Vincent, 1983; Larzelere & Huston, 1980; Rettig & Bulboz, 1983).

10. Finally, totally open, uncensored communication appears more common in *distressed* than *nondistressed* relationships (Bienvenu, 1970; Levinger & Senn, 1967).

In conclusion, Markman (1979) had premarital couples engage in laboratory-based communication tasks and then experimentally followed them for 2½ years. His results clearly indicated that communication quality was directly related to marital satisfaction. Thus, researchers have established predictive evidence that communicational abilities influence (and perhaps are influenced by) marital quality. In sum, the experimental evidence is overwhelming: Communications skills is an area that all marital therapists simply cannot ignore.

## TARGETS OF COMMUNICATIONS INTERVENTIONS

The targets of communications interventions are both narrow (i.e., well-defined) and extensive (i.e., broad). For explanatory purposes, we have classified these targets into four major groupings: (a) basics of communication, (b) principles of communication, (c) nonverbal behaviors, and (d) molecular verbal behaviors. In working with most couples, practitioners will recognize a host of communications deficits. Although we would like to be able to prioritize the order in which interventions should be made, quite frankly, we find this an impossible task. The idiosyncratic communications strengths and weaknesses of each couple demand an individualized approach. Thus, our immediate concern with Couple A may be behavior "B," whereas our most pressing target of change with Couple C may be behavior "D." In all instances, however, our purpose is to facilitate the effective transmission of thoughts, feelings, needs, and desires.

### Basics of Communication

Long-term, intimate relationships demand a nonspecific valuing of one's partner. We believe this can actually be divided into three separate communications skills: (a) respect, (b) understanding, and (c) sensitivity.

*Respect.* Certainly, when we speak of respect, we are referring to an attitude wherein partners truly hold each other in high regard and consider one another to be unique and worthwhile individuals. Moreover, with this attitude, partners are willing to verbalize their respect or act on it in some other manner. Thus, it is not surprising to see respect enacted by a willingness to work on couple-related problems. In its most basic form, respect is demonstrated by an ability to listen and attend to one's partner. Clearly, this moves beyond attitude and crosses over into the realm of an active valuing and sincere appreciation.

*Understanding.* Similar to the above, understanding is a complex process. However, it also has its behavioral referents. Gottman, Notarius, Gonso, and Markman (1976) refer to "validation" as a means by which partners obtain confirming and clarifying information from one another. When confused, partners can be trained to make the simple statement, "I'm not sure I understand, could you go over that once more for me?" Overtly, this appears as a basic request for more information. More subtly, however, partners are implicitly saying, "I'm really trying to see this from your perspective." In fact, that is what understanding is all about—an ability to empathically know and comprehend what it is that one's partner is experiencing. Further, there is an acceptance of this experience. This does not mean that spouses are constantly in agreement with one another, but that they have legitimized each other's frames of reference. In essence, each individual knows that he/she has been "confirmed." That is, communicational meanings have been shared and individuals recognized and accepted.

*Sensitivity.* A key element in the communicational process is being aware of one's partner's needs. Unfortunately, this appears to be relatively difficult. Individuals are frequently so concerned with themselves that they fail to even recognize what the partner desires. In other instances, they simply do not take the time to hear their partner's needs. Finally, there are those couples who choose not to be sensitive to one another for fear that they will be taken advantage of. In all of these instances, the end result is the same—partners fail to recognize and/or meet each other's needs, thereby drifting further and further apart.

## Principles of Communication

There are a number of overriding communications issues that transcend more molecular forms of relating. We have classified these as general principles and separated them into four categories: (a) timeliness, (b) manners, (c) specification, and (d) mind reading.

*Timeliness.* Individuals must learn to communicate with one another in a timely manner. This means that if there is something to be discussed between partners, it should be done expeditiously. Communication is enhanced when matters of both positive and negative valence are dealt with in a contemporaneous manner. Obviously, there are exceptions to this rule. For example, if a spouse were to come home drunk late one night, attempting to carry on meaningful conversation and discuss the matter would probably be a waste of effort. Under such circumstances, we would advise that the issue be addressed at some later, although not distant, point in time (e.g., the following morning). Similarly, partners must learn to express positive comments and reinforcing remarks at the time when a pleasant event occurs. To delay such statements rarely is of service to the relationship.

*Marital Manners.* One of the most revealing findings in the marital therapy literature has to do with differences in interaction between marital partners and strangers; namely, that when individuals interact in conversation with unknown adult strangers, they treat them in a gentler, more facilitative manner than they do their own spouses (Birchler et al., 1975; Vincent et al., 1975). They are more polite, provide greater social reinforcement, and engage in fewer disruptive interruptions with strangers than with their partners. The implications are clear. Most people know how to relate in a socially approved and proper manner, but, they often choose to be rude and boorish when interacting with their mates. As we have indicated in earlier chapters, this is exactly where the norm of reciprocity will prevail with distressed couples—nastiness will beget nastiness. Thus, although we wholeheartedly endorse the open expression of feeling, discourteous, ill-mannered, churlish communication will do considerably more harm than good.

*Behavioral Specification.* We have already discussed objectification as a major principle of relationship change. Furthermore, examples of behavioral specification have been provided in Chapter 4. However, behavioral specification is so important to effective communication that we have chosen to discuss it again in a slightly different manner.

When communicating in a behaviorally specific manner, individuals must accomplish three things. First, they must be able to pinpoint what it is they are feeling. Second, they must be able to specify how their partner's behavior is causally related to their feeling state. Third, they must be cognizant of the conditions under which their partner's behavior occurs. Gottman, Notarius, Gonso, & Markman (1976) have aptly described this process as the X-Y-Z formula: "I feel X, when you do Y in Z situation." To communicate effectively, couples simply must learn to adopt a paradigm similar to the Gottman et al. one. The more behaviorally specific individuals become, the higher the likelihood of providing useful information to one's partner and thereby resolving differences that may have arisen.

*Mind reading.* This is a process that refers to the belief that individuals know their partner's thoughts, feelings, or attitudes about some topic or event. That is, individuals *assume* they know how their spouses feel about something when, in point of fact, they may not know this at all. Of even greater importance is that negative mind reading differentiates distressed from nondistressed couples. This type of mind reading occurs when the attribution has a clear negative feeling associated with it (e.g., "He thinks I've handled this in a very childish and immature manner"). To circumvent negative mind reading, therapists need to instruct their clients in a "checking-out" procedure. This involves raising a series of questions to ascertain if information has been correctly understood. This is an excellent strategy for effectively relieving any misconceptions that partners may have about one another.

*Hank:* Jo, there's something I wanted to mention. When we go over to the Parkers' this weekend, let's be sure we don't monopolize the conversation. Okay?

*Jo: (angrily)* What the hell is that supposed to mean?

*Therapist:* Whoa! What's going on here? *(to Jo)* You're sounding real angry, real quick. Anger may certainly be okay, but you first might want to "check out" to make sure you understood what Hank was saying.

*Jo:* Yeah, that sounds like a good idea. *(to Hank)* What did you mean by that statement about not monopolizing the conversation? Do you think I talk too much or something?

*Hank:* No, not at all. I just meant that there are going to be some new people there, and I'd like to get to know them. If we do all the talking, they'll get to know us but we won't get to know very much about them. That's all I meant.

*Jo:* Oh, okay. I've got no problem with that. In fact, we've talked about trying to get to know some new people.

*Therapist: (to Jo)* But you did have a problem at first, didn't you?

*Jo:* Yeah, at first I thought he was accusing me of talking too much or was just afraid that I might say the wrong thing and embarrass him or something.

*Hank:* Wow! I guess I could have said it better in the first place. I didn't realize you'd take it like that.

*Jo:* Yeah, but I shouldn't have jumped on you quite the way I did. I've got to do that "checking out" before I immediately assume I know what's going on in your head.

*Hank:* It's simple. Just remember, there's usually nothing going on in my head. *(both laugh)*

## Nonverbal Behaviors

Research in the area of communications generally indicates that, when presented with contradictory verbal and nonverbal messages, individuals generally give greater credibility to the nonverbal aspects of the interaction (Stuart, 1980). In fact, nonverbal signals may convey upwards of 75% of the information people receive from others (Mehrabian, 1972). As a consequence, it is essential that therapists pay close attention to the nonverbal aspects of couples' interactions. In so doing, therapists can not only gain a fuller understanding of their clients, but also aid in clarifying communication and creating greater congruence between verbal and nonverbal forms of relating.

There is no doubt that facial expression is the most communicative aspect of human nonverbal behavior (Ekman & Friesen, 1969). Via facial expression, individuals communicate interest, agreement, anger, distrust, and hundreds of other human emotions. Unfortunately, there is not a direct correspondence between each of the emotions and facial expressions. However, general affects, attitudes, and beliefs certainly can be communicated between partners by a mere raising of the eyebrow. With respect to interpreting facial cues, therapists will want to pay particular attention to eyes, eye contact, head nods, smiles, frowns, and grimaces. Indeed, couples often develop highly idiosyncratic nonverbal forms of communication. These must be explored individually to ascertain their meaning.

We would like to briefly comment upon a few other significant nonverbal behaviors. First, voice tone clearly adds meaning to the content of an individual's message. Therapists might be especially interested in listening for monotonous versus modulated speech, dull versus enthusiastic, loud versus soft, and so on. Second, body language does communicate. Do partners face one another? What kinds of postures do they assume? How do they use their bodies for gestural purposes? These are all significant pieces of information that should be integrated into the course of therapy. Finally, therapists should observe clients' use of hands. Do partners touch one another? Is their touch friendly, helpful, patronizing, or aggressive? Can touching be employed as a means of therapeutically demonstrating care and concern? There are literally hundreds of nonverbal behaviors that individuals use to communicate with one another. Our primary concern is not with the behaviors per se, but with the communications process generally. Practitioners must understand and use that process to its fullest therapeutic advantage. Clearly, however, this will sometimes involve a focusing on discrete nonverbal behaviors in particular.

## Molecular Verbal Behaviors

There appear to be some very specific, discrete behaviors that individuals emit that either facilitate or impede the process of communication. Although there is general agreement regarding which behaviors facilitate and which behaviors impede, this does not indiscriminately apply across all couples. Thus, practitioners must observe individual couples' interactions and independently assess the effect that one partner's behavior has upon the other. In those instances, for example, where Spouse A raises her voice and Spouse B stops talking, it would appear that communication has ceased. Alternatively, Spouse C may raise her voice to Spouse D, and he may immediately ask, "My goodness, what have I done that's gotten you so upset?" She, in turn, responds in a very behaviorally specific manner, and it would appear that communication has been promoted. Because of this, readers must be cautious regarding the manner in which they use the information presented in Table 5.1. This table provides a listing of ten common positive and negative molecular verbal behaviors often exhibited by couples. Obviously, behaviors that facilitate communication are to be reinforced and promoted. Those that impede communication become immediate targets for change. During the course of therapy, practitioners will want to pay close attention to these and other behaviors that influence the communications process specifically and marital satisfaction generally.

# COMMUNICATIONS
# SKILLS TRAINING

The acquisition and maintenance of specific behavioral skills is significantly related to one's psychological well-being (Phillips, 1978). Skills training programs are therefore aimed at both increasing task-specific performance and general competency in a variety of life situations. As indicated by Goldsmith and McFall (1975), skills training programs emphasize the positive educational aspects of treatment. "Thus, when an individual's best effort is judged to be maladaptive, this indicates the presence of a situation-specific skill deficit in the individual's repertoire" (Goldsmith & McFall, 1975, p. 51). As we have indicated earlier, the communications deficits that occur among couples tend to be very situation specific; that is, they do not occur in conversations with unknown adults, and they are more apt to occur during attempted conflict-resolution discussions. Whatever the origin of the deficit (e.g., emotional upset, misattribution, past reinforcement history, etc.), appropriate training in the acquisition of

Table 5.1. Listing of 10 Positive and Negative Molecular Verbal Behaviors

| Behaviors that Facilitate Couples' Communication | Behaviors that Impede Couples' Communication |
|---|---|
| Be positive ("I like the way you . . . ") | Nagging |
| Be flexible | Interrupting |
| Be brief | Catastrophizing |
| Be assertive | Arguing over trivial matters |
| Be nondefensive | Overgeneralizing (e.g., using terms like |
| Personalize remarks (i.e., "I" statements) | "always" and "never") |
| State agreements when they occur | Sidetracking (i.e., getting off the subject) |
| Voice appreciation | Demanding/threatening |
| Express affection | Insulting |
| Use "measured" rather than "brutal" | Sarcasm |
| honesty | Hurtful criticism |

skillful responses should aid in developing more effective communications behavior for couples.

Communication skills are specific abilities. They are necessary so that an individual can perform competently when engaged in the symbolic transfer of messages from one person to another (i.e., spouse to spouse). McFall (1982) has indicated that competence is a relativistic evaluation, where performance on some task is judged to be competent or incompetent according to implicit or explicit criteria employed by judges. "In short, *there can be no absolute definition of a competent response, since competence inherently involves relativistic value judgments*" (McFall & Dodge, 1982, p. 361). Thus, it is the clinician who evaluates the behavior. More fully, he/she determines the situations, tasks, skills, and/or skill deficits that are consistently associated with the couples' communications difficulties. Certainly, the couples' values will influence the decision of how and when to intervene. Nonetheless, the major responsibility for intervention does lie with the clinician. Moreover, if progress is to be attained, this responsibility cannot be abandoned.

## Clinical Strategies of Communications Skills Training

Regardless of theoretical orientation, communications training is a widely accepted component of most marital treatment programs. However, the communications skills program described in this section differs from other treatment programs in a number of respects. First, as is true of most behavioral programs, the paradigm is flexibly but systematically applied. Second, the process follows directly from the material presented up to this point in the book. Thus, the applied techniques of relationship change form the basis of "how" to intervene, and the targets of communications interventions detail "where" to intervene. In essence, the communications skills training program is applied within the framework of our previously described behavioral-communication treatment model (Chapter 2). Third, the purpose of the program is to teach more effective communications skills and to facilitate the resolution of couples' conflicts. Consequently, we envision the program as being psychoprophylactic in nature. This will be discussed in greater detail in Chapter 7.

As should now be apparent, the training of specific skills follows directly from a comprehensive yet practical assessment. This assessment will generally indicate the idiosyncracies of the individual couple. Although our communications skills training program uses a sequence of clinical strategies, we do not conceive of it as an indiscriminately applied treatment package. In our opinion, such application cannot possibly meet the individual needs of the couple. Thus, we regard the communications skills training program as a "template" rather than a therapeutic "blueprint" for application. The component parts of this template are as follows: (a) instructions, (b) modeling, (c) rehearsal, (d) reinforcement, (e) feedback/ coaching, (f) rehearsal, and (g) homework. We will now very briefly review each of these strategies.

*Instructions.* This component simply involves telling the clients what exactly is expected of them. Although instructions are usually provided in a behaviorally specific manner, there may be occasions when the clinician will want to be purposely vague. This would occur if he/she were interested in assessing a couple's ability to resolve some area of disagreement with minimal direction from the therapist. In addition, there are some clients who appear to resent any formal direction from the therapist. In these instances, verbal instruction should probably be kept to a minimum. With most couples, however, the provision of a master cognitive set is usually of some assistance. Above all, the clinician must remember that the process of change is more apt to result from the experiential rather than intellectualized aspects of therapy. Thus, the purpose of instructions is not to provide insight, but to generate alternate, more effective ways of relating.

*Modeling.* This is a well-known psychological procedure with a demonstrated history of effectiveness (Bandura, 1969). Its primary usefulness with couples results from the observation of different forms of communication. In its most basic form, modeling entails the therapist playing the role of one member of the marital dyad in interaction with the other partner. Early in therapy, the therapist may actually complete the entire interaction while his/her role counterpart observes. As treatment progresses, however, the therapist is more apt to provide initial role-model comments and then quickly replace himself/herself with the actual partner. This occurs as clients become more and more proficient at generating effective ways of relating. As a consequence, less and less structure/direction is required by the therapist.

As noted by Jacobson and Margolin (1979), modeling may be even more effectively employed when two therapists are present. Under this circumstance, a number of role-playing variations are possible. Some of these would include:

1. Therapists can jointly model effective husband/wife behavior.
2. Therapists can model husband or wife behavior, taking turns engaging in the role-play with one of the spouses.
3. Therapists can speak directly to one another, modeling more effective communication strategies.
4. One therapist can model husband or wife behavior, while the other therapist continues in the role of therapist.
5. Therapists can "double" with husband and wife so that each role is being enacted by one therapist and one client.

Obviously, the combinations and permutations are almost endless. Therapists must be cautious, however, not to unwittingly create a countertherapeutic alliance. Striving for an equal amount of modeling and allowing for discussion following each enactment should circumvent this potential problem. In general, we have found modeling procedures to be enormously effective in initiating changes in couples' communication behaviors.

*Rehearsal.* "Behavioral rehearsal is a procedure whereby more desirable responses to interpersonal conflict situations are practiced under the supervision of the therapist" (Eisler & Hersen, 1973, p. 112). In couples' therapy, rehearsal clearly forms the core of communications skills training. It does so because it actually gives individuals the opportunity to put into practice that which they have observed and/or been instructed in. The therapist closely monitors this rehearsal and may provide small comments as the interaction continues (e.g., "good," "keep going," "that's fine," etc.). If, however, the clients get sidetracked or begin engaging in some destructive process, the therapist will probably want to terminate the rehearsal before matters entirely deteriorate. In either case, clinical strategies that follow rehearsal will then be implemented.

*Reinforcement.* Quite simply, immediately following behavioral rehearsal, clients should be socially reinforced for any approximation of the desired response. Once again, the therapist will want to attempt to provide an equal number of reinforcing comments to both the husband and wife. If the rehearsal was a complete failure, a number of alternatives may be entertained. First, the therapist may still want to reinforce where appropriate (e.g., "You folks really did a good job enacting your roles"). Second, he/she may simply want to move on to the next component in the communications skills training program. Third, the therapist may consider using the "internal dialogue" technique to see if he/she can figure out what it is that is happening in therapy right now. Fourth, ask the clients to do a "re-take" (this alternative is probably only appropriate if the therapist has reason to believe that the last rehearsal was totally unrepresentative). In most instances, some positive behaviors will have occurred and social reinforcement can then be appropriately applied. Because most rehearsals leave room for improvement, however, movement to the next step is usually required.

*Feedback/Coaching.* After having socially reinforced the couple for improvements in communications behaviors, the therapist will want to also provide some descriptive comments about the rehearsal. One must be careful here not to appear critical yet still remain informative (e.g., "John, I noticed you became very quiet once Eve started talking about her parents"). This type of feedback will usually generate some discussion from the couple regarding what they individually may have been thinking about during the rehearsal. This discussion can be very useful. The therapist may then choose to use this information as part of his/her coaching suggestion (e.g., "Well, John, if you think in-laws really aren't the problem, maybe you want to tell that to Eve next time she brings them up"). In addition, feedback regarding both verbal and nonverbal behavior is fair game. Once again, all therapist remarks should be conceptualized within the relationship (e.g., "I noticed you started smiling when you wife began talking about the trip to San Francisco"). Because this is not individual therapy, interventions should be focused upon the dyad and their transactions rather than the individual and his/her intrapsychic process.

*Rehearsal.* Having provided feedback/coaching, the therapist will then request that the couple once again engage in the communications process. Observations are then conducted in an effort to see if behavioral changes ensue. Clearly, the therapist is engaged in a shaping process, and further rehearsals will be required until more effective communications skills are behaviorally enacted by the couple. When such repeated rehearsals are necessary, any of the previously mentioned clinical strategies (e.g., instructions, modeling, etc.) may also be repeated. Behavior need not be perfect, but communication must be substantially more competent and interpersonally less painful than prior to the initiation of training.

*Homework.* Learning new communications skills in the presence of a therapist is a relatively safe environment. Eventually, however, these skills must be enacted by the couple without the aid of a therapist. Thus, once some degree of proficiency has been attained with each component skill, couples are usually given graded homework assignments. This requires considerable clinical skill. One does not want to require homework assignments beyond the skill level of the couple. Alternatively, the assignment should be relevant yet sufficiently difficult to be both challenging and rewarding. Although there are some standard assignments that are typically provided (e.g., caring days lists), most homework is distinctively constructed based upon the case conceptualization, course of therapy, and areas of continued conflict/disagreement. Some of these assignments may be the direct outgrowth of recent therapy meetings; other assignments may be paradoxical or intended to set the stage for later treatment sessions (Palazzoli-Selvini, Boscolo, Cecchin, & Prata, 1978). This will be discussed further in Chapters 7 and 8.

## Edited Transcript of Communications Skills Training

> *Therapist:* Cal, I can't help but notice that when you talk to Beth in here, you always refer to her in the third person rather than talking directly to her. Because one of the things that we're working on is direct communication, why don't you try speaking to her directly? (*Instructions*)
>
> *Cal:* Okay, like I was saying, she never seems able to. . . . (*Rehearsal*)
>
> *Therapist:* (*interrupts*) You mean Beth?
>
> *Cal:* Right. Beth never seems able. . . . (*Rehearsal*)
>
> *Therapist:* No, I want you to speak directly to Beth. (*Instructions*) Here, let me help. Why don't you look directly at Beth and say to her, "You never seem able to. . . . " All right, let's give that a try. (*Modeling*)
>
> *Cal:* Yeah, I think I've got it. Beth, what bothers me is that you never seem able to finish things that you start. You always leave things hanging and then expect me to finish them for you. (*Rehearsal*)
>
> *Therapist:* Okay, Beth, I'm sure you want to get in there and respond, but let me say just a couple of quick things. Cal, that was much better! You looked directly at Beth when you spoke, and that was really excellent. In fact, when you talked to her, you referred to her by name and then you spoke directly to her, not about her—that was great. (*Reinforcement*) However, I did notice that even though you spoke to her directly, she was getting pretty uneasy about what you were saying. Isn't that the case, Beth? (*Feedback*)
>
> *Beth:* Definitely. (*to Cal*) I don't like it when you make those sweeping generalizations.
>
> *Therapist:* (*to Beth*) What do you mean? Tell Cal.
>
> *Beth:* (*to Cal*) When you say I *never* finish things and *always* leave things for you, that's not true. There are some things that I start and don't finish, but not that many things, and I certainly don't leave everything for you.

*Therapist:* That's a good point. (*Reinforcement*) Cal, let's try talking directly to Beth again, but this time, rather than saying "always" and "never," maybe you'd be better off giving her a recent example or two of when this kind of thing has happened. (*Coaching*)

*Cal:* Okay. (*to Beth*) Last week, you started stripping the paint on the bathroom cabinets. You worked on it for about 3 hours Saturday afternoon and then you just left it and you haven't been back to it since. It sure doesn't look like it's going to get done soon and that's the kind of thing that's upsetting to me. (*Rehearsal*)

*Therapist:* Good.

*Beth:* I'm not asking you to finish it.

*Cal:* No, I didn't say you were.

*Beth:* Well, you said it before.

*Therapist:* Yes, but he's not saying that now. All he's saying now is that this job was started and it doesn't look like it's getting done. (*to Beth*) What do you say?

*Beth:* He's right.

*Therapist:* No, you're right. (*pointing to Cal; Coaching*)

*Beth:* Oh, yeah. You're right. I could definitely finish it off with another 6 hours worth of work, and I really should finish it. How about if I do 3 hours tonight and three hours on Saturday morning?

*Cal:* Well, you don't need my approval. I'll just be happy if it doesn't get left undone.

*Beth:* Okay, you've got my word. I'll finish by this weekend for sure.

*Therapist:* How do you both feel about that?

*Cal/Beth:* (Describe their pleasure at being able to settle the issue in a reasonable and efficient manner.)

*Therapist:* I'd like to give you a little homework, not with respect to getting jobs done, but with respect to communicating directly with one another. You got a real good start on it in here today. Now I want you to go home and make sure that you talk *directly* to one another at least 15 minutes per day, every day, until our next meeting. Can you do that? (*Homework*)

*Cal/Beth:* Sure, no problem.

*Therapist:* All right, but remember, you've got to look directly at one another—none of this third person junk. Plus, so that I can get a good idea of how the conversations went, I want you to keep a little notebook and write down when you talked, what you talked about, and how well you did with respect to talking directly to one another. Okay, can you guys do that?

*Cal/Beth:* Yup!

*Therapist:* All right, I'll see you next week, and I'll be real interested in looking at the little notebook along with you.

This transcript is rather self-explanatory. The therapist tried to balance interventions across husband and wife. Further, the "unfinished jobs" issue served as a vehicle for the facilitation of more effective communications skills (i.e., talking directly to one another). In addition, the homework assignment provided ample opportunity for transfer of therapeutic gains outside the therapy room. Upon returning the following week, the first item on the therapist's agenda was to go over the notebook and assignment with the couple.

## SUMMARY

Communications was initially defined as the symbolic means by which individuals transmit messages. Evidence was then presented indicating that communications deficits are central to the occurrence of marital distress. Subsequently, ten major applied research findings in the communications area were reviewed. The targets for communications interventions were then classified into four major groupings: (a) basics of communication, (b) principles of communication, (c) nonverbal behaviors, and (d) molecular verbal behaviors. The communications skills program was described by detailing each of the component parts: (a) instructions, (b) modeling, (c) rehearsal, (d) reinforcement, (e) feedback/coaching, (f) rehearsal, and (g) homework. Explanation was provided indicating that the communications skills program is applied within the framework of the previously described behavioral-communications treatment model. The chapter closed with a verbatim, edited transcript of a communications skills training session.

# Chapter 6
# Problem-Solving Training*

The behavioral-communications model thus far presented has primarily focused on principles of relationship change in general and communications skills training in particular. Indeed, these are considered first-order, essential components of the program. However, couples typically enter therapy with both pervasive complaints and raw, unresolved conflicts. Although behavior change tactics and skills training procedures will frequently increase the "positiveness" of the relationship, a series of unresolved conflicts may remain. Enter problem-solving training! The major intent of this procedure is to teach couples to negotiate equitable solutions to their problem situations. Most interesting, though, is that although the technique is used to resolve content-related differences, it is the *process* of resolving these differences that is of paramount importance. Thus, although effective problem-solving does result in a mutually agreed upon solution, it is the means to the achievement of this solution that is of greatest concern to the behavioral-communications marital therapist. As a consequence, virtually any problem that requires negotiation can serve as an effective instrument for the learning of conflict resolution skills. This is exceptionally important to distressed couples for a number of reasons. First, negative reciprocity is particularly apt to occur in conflict situations. Even if the relationship is improving as a result of treatment, conflicts will, no doubt, serve as real impediments to continued progress. Second, as we indicated earlier, distressed and nondistressed couples differ markedly in their ability to settle matters of dispute (Gottman, 1979). Major areas of disagreement must therefore become an active source of concern for all marital therapists. Finally, problem-solving training clearly has the potential for serving a preventive function, because the future conflicts of couples are bound to arise. Once clients have been trained and can effectively implement problem-solving skills, they, in essence, become their own therapists. We will return to this issue in the next chapter, but let

---

*Portions of this chapter are based upon an earlier report by Bornstein, Fisher, and Balleweg (1982).

us now briefly examine some of the literature in the area of problem-solving training.

## A BRIEF HISTORY
## OF THE PROCEDURE

During the past decade, behavioral interventions have been increasingly applied to the alleviation of marital distress (Gurman & Kniskern, 1978). In so doing, behavioral marital therapists have utilized a behavior exchange model of interaction (Linehan & Rosenthal, 1979), viewing marital discord as a product of overreliance on aversive control strategies (Weiss, 1978). Within this framework, therapy has been designed to decrease reciprocal rates of aversive behaviors while simultaneously increasing dyadically based forms of positive reinforcement (Jacobson & Martin, 1976).

One of the primary techniques employed using the behavior exchange treatment model has been behavioral problem-solving. As commonly practiced, problem-solving involves a structured set of interactions designed to resolve specific areas of conflict between partners (Jacobson & Margolin, 1979). The importance of training couples in effective problem-solving skills has been amply demonstrated by Vincent et al. (1975). These researchers found that distressed married couples exhibited significantly fewer positive and more negative problem-solving behaviors than non-distressed couples. In addition, a wide variety of investigations have used problem-solving training to successfully treat marital discord (Bornstein, Anton et al., 1981; Bornstein, Bach et al., 1981; Jacobson, 1977, 1978, 1979; Weiss, Hops, & Patterson, 1973). Jacobson (1977), for example, successfully treated a group of 10 distressed couples with a package comprised of problem-solving training and contingency contracting procedures. In a subsequent study (Jacobson, 1979), this same investigator was able to produce positive changes in the home, as reported by spouses, in four of six severely distressed couples through the use of a problem-solving strategy. More recently, Bornstein and his associates have demonstrated the effectiveness of a combined problem-solving and communications training program in the alleviation of marital distress when treatment focused either on increases in positive (Bornstein, Anton et al., 1981) or decreases in negative interactions (Bornstein, Hickey et al., 1983).

Collectively, these previously cited investigations provide substantial empirical support for the effectiveness of problem-solving approaches in the treatment of marital discord. Although future research must further define the active parameters of such a problem-solving strategy, treatment integrity (Yeaton & Sechest, 1981) demands a behaviorally specific intervention protocol. Moreover, given the minimal amount of training in marital therapy provided by most graduate programs in psychology (Prochaska & Prochaska, 1978), clinicians clearly require greater familiarization with these efficacious procedures. Thus, in the remaining sections of this chapter, we will: (a) provide a brief conceptualization of marital conflict resolution, (b) present a heuristic, step-by-step guide for couples' problem-solving behaviors, (c) address the clinical implications of such an approach, and (d) give a brief case example.

# CONCEPTUALIZATION
# OF MARITAL CONFLICT AND
# ITS RESOLUTION

Training couples in systematic problem-solving makes an implicit statement about conflict and its occurrence. Simply stated, when two people live together as a couple, conflict will arise. By the very nature of couples' interactions, there will be times when either disagreements occur and/or needs go unmet. As a result, partners will feel angry, frustrated, and dissatisfied with one another. Thus, if conflict is to arise, couples should be prepared for it; not only in terms of ability to communicate effectively, but also with regard to the implementation of a systematic problem-solving strategy that affords structure and order to conflict resolution sessions.

Before detailing the specific steps in conflict resolution, however, there are a few overriding concerns that warrant mentioning. First, as has already been implied, effective problem-solving demands effective communication skills. As a consequence, we advise that marital therapists who employ the problem-solving program detailed in the following section do so in conjunction with, or immediately following, the training of couples in dyadic communications skills (see Chapter 5). Second, within the relationship, we conceive of all conflicts as *couple* conflicts rather than individual problems, because conflicts are, by definition, mutual in nature. The effect of such a philosophy is to create an atmosphere wherein problem-solving is not to help one partner or the other, but rather to help the relationship. Finally, the object of problem-solving is not to prove one spouse right or the other spouse wrong. The object is to solve the problem and arrive at a workable solution that is mutually acceptable to all parties concerned. This is not an easy task and requires a concerted effort by both spouses and therapist.

Finally, similar to Jacobson and Margolin (1979), we divide problem-solving into two distinct phases: (a) identifying the problem, and (b) solving the problem. In the first phase, individuals are working toward developing a mutual understanding of the problem. A variety of skills are required at this point. Namely, partners must be capable of behavioral

MT-D*

specification, expression of feeling, and active listening skills (all topics previously discussed). In the latter phase, choosing and enacting a solution will be of prime concern. Consequently, brainstorming, compromise, and evaluation skills will be of higher priority. Needless to say, different skills will be required at different times. Quite frankly, we find this division of problem-solving into two separate phases quite helpful. First, it provides clients with a clear specification of task. They know that during Phase I, the job is to adequately define the problem. During Phase II, they are to arrive at an agreement. Thus, they very quickly learn that discussing solutions during Phase I or further defining the problem during Phase II is highly inappropriate. Of course, it may require a statement on the part of the therapist to remind them of this. Second, by dividing into phases, couples experience a sense of success as they work through the program, even though they may have not yet reached an acceptable solution. They can, however, recognize the progress that has been achieved and the remaining steps that lie before them. Finally, many couples are truly fearful of attempting to solve differences of opinion. Their past history has taught them that the process is apt to become hurtful and ugly. By structuring problem-solving into two distinct phases with a variety of subphases, the therapist implicity suggests that this new process will be both orderly and controlled. For many this provides a sense of relief, independent of the yet-to-be-achieved conflict resolution. With this in mind, the program presented in the following section attempts to organize problem-solving efforts for both in-session and home use. Clearly, as we saw with communications training, progress should first be obtained with the therapist present before assignment is given for extra-therapy implementation.

## COUPLES' GUIDE TO
## PROBLEM-SOLVING

### Identifying the Problem (Steps 1-3)

*Step 1: Choosing an Appropriate Time and Place for Problem-solving.* This step obviously should not present any difficulties for in-session problem-solving. It is assumed that the regularly scheduled therapy hour and the therapist's office are highly appropriate setting conditions for problem-solving. However, with respect to home problem-solving, it must be recognized that this process cannot be done anywhere, at any time. In order to constructively discuss areas where there are clear differences of opinion, spouses will need some privacy. Thus, before even attempting to work out a solution to some problem, couples must first find an environment that facilitates a frank discussion of the issues at hand. In conjunction with this, the time for such problem-solving must also be appropriate. Consequently, couples must learn not to discuss sexual dissatisfactions in the final 15 minutes before leaving for work in the morning. In addition, they will want to consider delaying topics for discussion when one or both partners are obviously emotionally upset. Trying to problem-solve under such circumstances usually causes more harm than good.

*Step 2: Recording the "Vitals" of Problem-solving Sessions.* When problems are discussed and solutions achieved, one or both partners in the dyad agree to change their behavior in some way. This is a commitment. If commitments are made, they should be followed. Thus, it is essential that individuals have a record of commitments offered by one another during their problem-solving sessions. Therefore, we require that a record of all vital information from the problem-solving session be recorded in a couple's notebook. Table 6.1 illustrates what such a notebook might look like. There are four major pieces of information recorded: Date, Problem Discussed, Outcome Achieved, and Initials. The information in the first three columns is briefly recorded and then initialed by participating parties. This insures that both individuals involved in the problem-solving agree as to what has been discussed and the outcome achieved. There is no need to rely on memory, and the recording process itself undoubtedly serves as a cue to behavior change. Although information should be recorded in rather specific terms, a couple's experience is probably the best judge

Table 6.1. Problem-Solving Notebook

| Date | Problem Discussed | Outcome Achieved | Initials |
|---|---|---|---|
| 4/27/85 | Chris upset with Ray for falling asleep after dinner on almost 50% of the week-nights for the past month. | Chris commits herself to allowing Ray 15 minutes rest before dinner; Ray promises to remain alert and socially engaged until bedtime. | CH-RH |
| 5/10/85 | Ray and Chris both agree that they would like to meet and socialize with some new people. | Ray and Chris will join a bowling league and begin attending at least two church socials per month. | CH-RH |
| 5/23/85 | Ray complains about sexual boredom; he would like to engage in some new and exciting sexual activities with Chris. | Chris volunteers to initiate new sexual intercourse positions at least twice during the next month; Ray consents to trying mutual masturbation techniques in addition to intercourse. | CH-RH |

in matters such as this. That is, if one spouse fails to carry out his/her commitment because of a misunderstanding, a more explicit description of "outcome achieved" may be required at later problem-solving sessions.

*Step 3: Being Specific in Defining the Problem.* As we have repeatedly stressed, behavioral specification may well be the most important concept in all of behavioral-communications marital therapy. Within the area of problem-solving, such specification is best accomplished by using the X-Y-Z paradigm we earlier discussed: "I feel X when you do Y in Z situation" (Gottman, Notarius, Gonso, & Markman, 1976). Vague, long-winded analyses of "why" the problem occurs tend to be quite useless. Instead, specific, direct, task-oriented examples of the problem behavior are apt to be truly facilitative of conflict resolution. Although partners will want to get their point across, the therapist must remind them that the intention is not to hurt or offend, but rather to problem-solve. Thus, even though individuals may be upset, they will still want to take their partner's feelings into consideration and not create any undue antagonism by virtue of the manner in which issues are expressed.

In addition, a number of related matters bear some mentioning. First, it is generally recommended that partners refrain from focusing on the intention or supposed reason for their spouse's behavior. This type of mind reading tends to be quite unproductive and only leads to defensiveness and task-irrelevant verbal interaction. Instead, partners must be reminded to stick to the facts: "I feel X when you do Y in Z situation." Second, couples should attempt to discuss no more than one problem at a time. Moreover, that problem should be under the couple's control and presented in a manner that is solvable. This means that couples should be taught to confront problems that are presently occurring or could potentially develop in the near future. It makes no sense to discuss a problem that is long past or simply unsolvable. Finally, in defining the problem to be discussed, the therapist will want to take into consideration how well the therapy is progressing. That is, the couple should not be allowed to overextend themselves in the initial phases of treatment. Has the therapist begun to see the rewarding effects of behavioral exchange? Is communication improving? Are partners beginning to relate to one another in more positive ways? In most instances, the therapist should suggest that the couple will want to begin with small issues and work their way up toward the "biggies" when problem-solving. Once having achieved satisfactory resolution with regard to some of the lesser conflicts in the relationship, they can then feel free to gradually tackle the more significant problems that may exist.

# Solving the Problem (Steps 4-9)

*Step 4: Accepting the "Problem" and Moving Toward a Solution.* After one spouse has shared what he/she deems a problem, he/she will expect some response from his/her partner. What should be said? What should be done? To become good problem-solvers, individuals must first learn to listen to and accept their spouse's feelings. A feeling is an emotional reaction to a situation. It is sometimes rationally and sometimes irrationally based. It may be congruent with the other spouse's feelings, or it may be highly disparate. Feelings, however, are not right or wrong. Feelings are facts. They are an individual's response to his/her perceived reality. As such, they are not to be argued with but rather accepted as one of the three key elements in the problem-solving complex. Those elements, of course, include feelings (X), behaviors (Y), and situations (Z). All too often, couples involve themselves in the nonproductive vicious cycle of arguing with one another as to whether the feelings are correct or incorrect. This is apt to be a useless waste of couples' and therapists' time. Thus, to begin solving a problem, therapists will want to instruct individuals to first accept their spouse's feelings as accurate representations of his/her reality. Then, together they can jointly entertain the all-important question, *"What can be done about this?"*

*Step 5: Problem Solution First Requires Goal Specification.* Succinctly stated, if couples are going to solve their own problems, they must first know what they are working toward. Thus, goals must be concrete and stated in an explicit manner that allows for clear identification of whether they have or have not been achieved. In addition, spouses must reach agreement that the explicitly stated goal is, in fact, acceptable to both of them. Finally, the goal must be practical. There is no sense in explicitly stating goals and reaching agreement if the goal cannot be attained (e.g., getting a Ph.D. in clinical psychology within a one-year period of time). This is a meaningless expenditure of energy.

*Step 6: Considering the Broadest Range of Possible Solutions.* One of the most rewarding aspects of problem-solving is that it allows individuals to be creative in resolving difficulties that arise within their relationships. After having developed goals, partners should explore and give consideration to a wide variety of potential solutions to their problems. Of greatest significance, individuals must be totally open-minded regarding the generation of possible alternatives. At this point in the process, the couple should not rule out any potential forms of resolution. In fact, brainstorming (i.e., considering the widest range of possible solutions to the problem) is the order of the day. This, of course, is to be implemented without regard to evaluation. Couples should be creative, generate solutions, and list them all, no matter how outlandish they may first appear. Later, these ideas can be rationally evaluated, but initially the therapist wants to get potential solutions to simply flow freely. Record keeping may be particularly useful at this point. Thus, it is recommended that couples record all solutions generated during the brainstorming phase.

*Step 7: Choosing a Solution with Compromise in Mind.* Once the couple has completed the brainstorming list, they are ready to begin the selection of one or more alternative solutions to the problem. The therapist's first task will be to aid the couple in eliminating the obviously inadequate solutions. After this is accomplished, remaining solutions can be eliminated on the bases of solution practicality, coincidence with values, and cost-benefit analyses. Practicality refers to whether the alternative can be realistically implemented. Coincidence with values is related to whether the solution is in keeping with the couple's value system. Finally, a cost-benefit analysis enables the partners to estimate how much effort is involved in implementing the solution and determining the likelihood of achieving the stated goal.

The notion of cost-benefit analysis is directly related to the major function of Step 7. In attempting to analyze the various solutions, it will soon become apparent that the various costs and benefits will be different for each of the individuals in the relationship; that is, one solution may involve a minimal amount of effort for Partner A, maximal effort for Partner B, and high likelihood of goal achievement for the couple. On the other hand, another solution may yield the total converse (i.e., maximal effort for Partner A, minimal effort for Partner B, goal achievement for the couple). How do partners decide which solution ought to be implemented? The answer lies in the art of compromise. To achieve the very best solutions to most couples' problems, both partners will want to learn to modify their positions to the extent that they accommodate the needs of their spouses as well as themselves.

*Step 8: Trying It Out, Collecting Data, and Evaluating the Outcome.* Once the solution has been chosen, mutually agreed to by both parties, and recorded in the problem-solving diary, it should be enacted. If "outcome achieved" has been recorded in behaviorally specific terms, it is a simple task to collect information that can later be used to evaluate the solution. Is each party carrying out the tasks as committed? Are tasks being accomplished in a timely manner? Are the various activities taking place in their proper environments? Questions such as these demand behaviorally observable criteria that should be part of both the data recording and collection system. Thus, after giving the solution a fair trial of implementation (which, of course, will vary considerably depending upon the problem), the therapist and couple can then evaluate the results.

*Step 9: If Necessary, Refine, Revise, Renegotiate.* After having evaluated the outcome, couples will be ready to deal with the following questions: Are the achieved results satisfactory? Is it possible that better solutions exist within the context of the cost-benefit analysis? Will the present solution work effectively for some time into the future? Many couples find that although they are quite pleased with the results of their initial solution implementation, all is not perfect. This is fine. In fact, therapists and clients alike should not perceive this as failure. Instead, dissatisfaction should serve as an impetus to further problem-solving. Realistically, there are probably three levels of problem-solving that may occur at this time. At the first level, a couple's solution may need slight refinement, and minor adjustments in the solution should correct any difficulties that may have arisen. At the second level, adjustments tend to be a bit more substantial. Here, although parties stay with the same solution that was chosen earlier, an actual revision is required. Thus, the solution may change substantially in form and shape (e.g., cooking breakfast for one another daily versus going out to restaurants on weekdays). The final level is when a renegotiation is required. In this instance, the initial solution has been found unacceptable, and the couple will need to re-examine alternative solutions or generate new ones in their place. The therapist should impress upon the couple that none of these outcomes is more favorable than the other. Certainly, although it may be easier to simply accept the first solution as the best alternative, couples' satisfaction in general and goal attainment in particular are the prime considerations. In that respect, any avenue that allows for closer approximation of the desired goals must be considered a highly appropriate route.

## CLINICAL IMPLICATIONS

Improving problem-solving skills is only one of several possible therapeutic approaches available for the facilitation of effective couple interaction. Whereas other marital therapy techniques have typically emphasized the training of discrete responses in specific problem situations, the present training program was designed to create a "learning set." Clients must learn to efficiently deal with a variety of diverse conflict forms and to do so within a relatively self-administered format. Although the therapist initially provides considerable structure, clearly the goal of treatment is for couples to eventually become their own therapists. Moreover, the skills they develop can be applied to the broad range of problems that inevitably occur within long-term relationships.

The current problem-solving behavior guide also appears particularly well-suited to cope with both the immense variability of complaints and the many differing types of couples who often seek help. Because rather detailed instructions have been provided regarding therapist use, it is anticipated that application and evaluation may be facilitated. As empirical clinicians, we welcome this integration of our science and practice.

## A BRIEF CASE EXAMPLE
## OF PROBLEM-SOLVING

Mr. & Mrs. E (Mike and Gloria) had been married for 16 years at the time of referral. Mike, age 40, was employed as an accountant in a locally owned general construction firm, and Gloria, age 37, was a homemaker and part-time student at the university. Initial assessment indicated numerous areas of conflict (e.g., financial, family, and personal independence) and communications difficulties. Both Mike and Gloria tended to relate to one another in a demanding, caustic, and obstructionistic manner. Moreover, they were rarely able to reach agreement on matters of significant concern to the family. They had two children, both girls, ages 12 and 14.

Because our present concern is with problem-solving per se, we will not provide a detailed overview of this couple's marital therapy. However, it should be noted that a comprehensive yet practical assessment was conducted, and the first four sessions of treatment focused on mutually increasing positive behaviors and communications skills training. During the fifth session, however, a blending of communications and problem-solving training occurred. At this time, Gloria very reasonably stated to Mike: "I get very scared whenever I see you starting to lose control in your disciplining of the girls." Although the communications training had "paid off" to some extent (i.e., Gloria was brief, direct, expressive of feeling, etc.), the therapist aided her in formulating an even more detailed account via the use of an X-Y-Z formula. Her response to this involved a number of distinct features:

1. Gloria provided two recent examples of Mike's "loss of control," which were extremely well-specified.
2. Gloria's emphasis was neither overbearing nor demanding. She simply informed Mike of the kind of a reaction his behavior prompted in her (i.e., "I get very much afraid that you're either going to hurt them physically or say something that creates even greater harm").
3. Gloria further admitted that she probably had some role in the problem, because she tended to leave most of the disciplining to Mike.

4. Mike responded very nondefensively. He clearly indicated that he accepted Gloria's concern and that even though he did not feel "out of control" he could, in fact, understand how she might worry about this.

Mike and Gloria then defined the problem as: "We must find more effective, less threatening ways of disciplining the children." The therapist was quite pleased with this reformulation, because it now had obviously become more of a couple's, rather than an individual's problem. At this point, the therapy session was brought to a close, and both partners were given the independent homework assignment of brainstorming solutions to the problem. Upon returning the following week, proposed solutions included the following:

1. Mike disciplines the girls when Gloria is not in the house.
2. Mike stops disciplining entirely; Gloria assumes all disciplinary responsibility.
3. Mike pays no attention to Gloria's concern and continues to discipline as in the past.
4. The girls are sent away to boarding school.
5. The girls are sent to live with a relative in another city.
6. Gloria stops worrying about Mike's handling of the discipline.
7. Mike and Gloria divide the disciplinary responsibilities along some prearranged lines.
8. Mike and Gloria consult with one another before discipline occurs.
9. Mike and Gloria take a parent effectiveness class at the university.
10. Gloria allows Mike to continue to be the primary disciplinarian, but stops him whenever she feels as though he's losing control.

From this list, Mike and Gloria were able to immediately discard some obviously inadequate solutions. After further discussion and some refinement, they decided that Mike would be responsible for academic discipline and Gloria for home discipline. Further, before any disciplining occurred, they would attempt to consult with one another and reach agreement as to the manner in which it would be handled. Mike and Gloria recognized that under some circumstances immediate consultation was impossible. Accordingly, the responsible parent would take whatever expedient action was required and then consult with the other parent at his/her earliest convenience. This plan was approved by both Mike and Gloria and given a 2-week trial evaluation. Data were collected with regard to the number of disciplinary actions required and the other parent's degree of comfort with each such intervention.

Results were overwhelmingly positive. During the 2-week trial, Mike had disciplined the girls on only two occasions, and Gloria had reason to discipline them only three times. In all but one instance, they had the opportunity to consult with one another before disciplining. On the one other occasion, Gloria "grounded" the 12-year-old and later spoke to Mike about the punishment. He agreed entirely. Further, both parents rated their degree of comfort with each disciplinary effort at "100% agreement."

In sum, the problem-solving procedure had worked exceptionally well with this couple. In the remaining therapy sessions, problem-solving continued both in the office and at home. Advances occurred across other problem areas in the relationship (e.g., finances, personal independence, etc.), and both Mike and Gloria later commented on the remarkable improvement that had taken place in their ability to communicate and work out differences with one another.

## SUMMARY

Problem-solving involves a structured set of interactions designed to resolve specific areas of conflict between partners. Although the procedure focuses on negotiating agreements to content-related problems, it is the *process* of resolving differences that is of primary importance. A brief history of the problem-solving literature was presented along with a conceptualization of marital conflict and its resolution. Following these actions, a step-by-step guide for the instigation of couples' problem-solving was detailed. The format utilized employed two phases: (a) identifying and (b) solving the problem. Topics discussed in the first phase included choosing an appropriate time/place, record keeping, and specification. Later steps addressed issues related to problem acceptance, range of alternatives, compromise, evaluation, and revision. Subsequent to presentation of the guide, clinical implications and a brief case example were provided.

# Chapter 7
# Maintenance and Prevention

In the first six chapters of this book, our emphasis has clearly been remedial in nature. We have been discussing means by which practitioners can effectively modify *dysfunctional couples' behaviors* presently in existence. Thus, we address a new topic entirely when we begin considering procedures used to maintain *behavioral improvements* that have already been achieved as a result of treatment. Moreover, preventing problematic couples' interactions before they begin is a second topic quite distinct from our discussion of remediation. However, that is just the purpose of this chapter. We will first discuss the maintenance-enhancing strategies inherent in the behavioral-communications approach and then attempt to demonstrate how behavioral-communications principles can be easily incorporated into a prevention-based program.

## MAINTENANCE

The value of marital therapy lies not only in the remediation of couples' dysfunctions, but also in the maintenance and/or transfer of improvement across time, behaviors, and situations. Quite frankly, although the development of more effective relationship skills within the therapy room may be of some import, behavioral change simply must maintain beyond the time limits of the traditional 50-minute hour. Maintenance refers explicitly to improvements over time. Transfer of training (or generalization), on the other hand, deals with behavior change that extends across behaviors and situations. In the past, many explanations for maintenance and transfer failures have been speculative or post hoc in nature. Continued improvement was something hoped and prayed for rather than expected. Today, however, it is widely accepted that maintenance of behavior change must be systematically programmed into all comprehensive treatment regimes (Stokes & Baer, 1977). Such programming has been demonstrated to be an effective means of increasing the likelihood of maintenance and generalization following the termination of treatment.

Some of the methods found successful in promoting maintenance and generalization have been incorporated in the behavioral-communications treatment approach. The first section of this chapter will therefore highlight those technical procedures that address relevant issues of maintenance and transfer of training.

## Behavioral Traps

Behavioral traps refer to generating behaviors that will be naturally reinforced in the extratherapeutic environment (Baer, Rowbury, & Goetz, 1976; Baer & Wolf, 1970; Stokes & Baer, 1977). While in therapy, the client's behavior may be controlled by extraneous forces (e.g., therapist praise or therapist instruction), but the trap allows these behaviors to be maintained, because once established they are apt to be reinforced within the marital relationship.

Homework assignments can undoubtedly function as traps. For example, having couples complete the caring days homework assignment gives them the opportunity to please one another without formally expecting anything in return. However, the well-established norm of reciprocity clearly indicates that partners work toward a balance in the generation of pleasing behaviors. Thus, "if you do for me, I'm apt to do for you." *Voila*—herein lies the behavioral trap! Moreover, assignments such as these force partners to attend to and acknowledge what pleases their partners. This also is a trap, because, once acknowledged, the likelihood of generating partner-pleasing behaviors is greatly increased. In this manner, behavioral exchange procedures in general and most homework assignments in particular form a foundation of positive behaviors waiting to be reinforced in the natural environment.

## Fading of Contingencies

Losses of behavioral improvements over time often result from the abrupt withdrawal of reinforcing and punishing consequences. However, gradually removing or fading contingencies is less likely to be discernible by clients and therefore more likely to result in maintenance and generalization (Paul & Lentz, 1977; Phillips, Phillips, Fixsen, & Wolf, 1971; Turkewitz, O'Leary, & Ironsmith, 1975). Thus, behavioral-communications therapists purposefully reduce external consequences of behavior over the course of the therapeutic program. In so doing, the contingencies in effect at the time of termination closely resemble those consequences found in the natural environment.

This principle is exemplified in a number of behavioral-communications procedures. For example, it is expected that as therapy progresses, the clinician will intervene on a progressively less frequent basis. More responsibility is given to the couple as they are able to relate to one another in a more effective manner. The fading of treatment contingencies is also evinced via the intermittent scheduling of sessions over time. Generally speaking, couples are initially seen at 1-week intervals. This is eventually faded to once every other week, once per month, and so on. Finally, fading of contingencies also occurs within the communications skills program. Early in treatment, the therapist may model effective communication behaviors. Later, the therapist may give the words to the client, but the client actually speaks them. Subsequently, the therapist may *ask* the client to respond by himself/herself. Following this, the therapist may need to do no more than raise an eyebrow as a means of bringing forth the effective client response. Lastly, the client responds without any intervention on the part of the therapist. In sum, a fading of therapist involvement occurs as the couple becomes skilled at handling their own difficulties.

## Expanding Stimulus Control

When behaviors become associated with a narrow range of cues or settings, maintenance and transfer to new situations are not apt to occur. Thus, maintenance and transfer can be developed by widening the range of stimuli that exert control over the behavior (Emshoff, Redd, & Davidson, 1976; Stokes, Baer, & Jackson, 1974). In this instance, persons, settings, and times that are associated with effective couples' interactions are expanded to include extratherapy settings as well. Once again, homework assignments are typically employed to accomplish this purpose. Although homework assignments may not always be done at home (e.g., ''I'd like you two to go out and see an X-rated film together this week''), they certainly are not completed in the therapist's office or in the therapist's presence. In fact, they can be done almost anywhere and at any time, but not during therapy. Consequently, the treatment regime allows for generalization of newly learned skills to novel environments, different times, and different places.

## Self-Control

Behaviors that are under external stimulus control have a lower likelihood of transfer than those that are self-consequated. Thus, when clients are taught to monitor, evaluate, and reinforce their own performance, behavioral improvements are apt to be sustained over time and across settings

(Bornstein & Quevillon, 1976; Felixbrod & O'Leary, 1974). Because of the
better results, the behavioral-communications model attempts to train
couples to serve as their own therapists. Whenever possible, couples are
given the opportunity to solve their problems without the aid of the
therapist. In fact, the therapist only intervenes when the couple has fully demonstrated an inability to deal successfully with the situation themselves. Therefore, the skills developed in the therapy room eventually
come under the complete control of the couple. By learning to use these
techniques both inside and outside of therapy, couples then insure their
ability to evaluate and effectively deal with problems as they arise in the
natural environment. The likelihood of continued and enhanced relationship gains is thus even greater.

## Peer Facilitators

Research indicates that peers may be utilized to aid in maintenance and
generalization of newly learned behaviors (Johnston & Johnston, 1972;
Stokes & Baer, 1977). The literature on peer reinforcement, for example,
indicates that once peers are appropriately trained, they may continue to
provide reinforcement to their partners and serve as discriminative stimuli
to cue more effective behaviors (Greer & Polirstok, 1982). In marital therapy, what peer is more present than one's spouse? Furthermore, the behavioral-communications treatment program is conjoint in nature; that is,
individuals are seen together in treatment. Thus, each individual serves
as his/her partner's discriminative stimulus for the newly acquired positive
interactional behaviors.

Although maintaining behavioral improvements over time and across
settings is certainly important, preventing problems before they develop
must be considered an even higher ideal. It is to that topic that we now
turn.

## PREVENTION

In Chapter 1, we commented extensively upon the pervasiveness of distressed couples' relations. Our section on divorce statistics and factors influencing divorce lends credence and support to the already widely known
fact that living happily ever after only occurs in fairy tales. One of the
reasons for the high divorce rate is that a great many couples jump feet
first into marriage having had only the limited role-model training of their
parents. Undoubtedly, contemporary couples would be better able to live
*more* happily ever after had they first received some preventive training.
Such instruction could aid them in enhancing relationship satisfaction,
short-circuiting common couple-based difficulties, and dealing more effectively with everyday problems as they arise.

In the past, therapists have shown little interest in or commitment to prevention (Kessler & Albee, 1977; Klein & Goldston, 1977). Relatively speaking, as a mental health area, preventive research has not been actively pursued. In fact, prevention itself has been described as "more cost than benefit" (Cumming, 1972), "corraling a cloud" (Isbister, 1975), and "an illusion" (Henderson, 1975). Further, it would appear that these sentiments have been almost universally condoned within the ranks of psychotherapy in general, and marital therapy in particular.

Recently, however, increasing attention has been paid to the possibility of preventing marital distress (Ginsburg & Vogelsong, 1977; Markman & Floyd, 1980; Meadow & Taplin, 1970; Miller, Nunnally, & Wackman, 1975; Schlein, 1971). Quite succinctly, the position held by these authors is that prevention is better than cure. Methods are applied to specific populations in the present as a means of decreasing problematic and costly behavior in the future. We not only accept this position, but believe that it has application within a behavioral-communications model specifically. Thus, although the intent of this book is to aid professionals in their work with clinically distressed couples, we find the approach serves an auxiliary function as well—namely, as a tool for the prevention of marital distress.

We do not intend to review the prevention literature as it deals (or does not deal) with the topic of marital dysfunction. However, we will first describe the classical prevention subdivisions so as to provide the reader with an organized conceptual framework. Following this, an attempt will be made to integrate these concepts with the behavioral-communications treatment model presented throughout this book.

## Types of Prevention

It is generally agreed that there are three major forms of prevention: primary, secondary, and tertiary (Heller & Monahan, 1977). For our purpose, *primary prevention* refers to interventions aimed at couples not currently experiencing distress. Such interventions provide couples with resources that can be used to interrupt potential problems prior to their actual occurrence. In most instances, these interventions are directed toward transition and milestone periods in the life cycle of the relationship (e.g., engagement, marriage, birth of the first child, etc.). During these critical periods, stress is high, and the couple may need efficient coping strategies to effectively manage the relationship. Primary prevention programs serve just that purpose.

*Secondary prevention* is conceived as intervention directed toward those populations known to be at risk with respect to relationship difficulties. These at-risk couples are identified via systematic assessment and diagnostic procedures (see Chapter 3). The aim of secondary prevention is to focus on problems in the relationship in an attempt to decrease their severity through early intervention. *Tertiary prevention*, on the other hand, is directed toward those couples who have already experienced severe problems in order to reduce the likelihood of their recurrence. Obviously, these couples are quite vulnerable to relapse and/or continued distress.

The majority of psychological interventions typically have secondary or tertiary preventive properties. Thus, with couples, therapists generally apply treatment once the distress is already reported. In fact, prediction efforts can provide probability estimates regarding the development of the relationship distress in groups of couples, but these data have generally not been demonstrated to accurately predict individually distressed couples. Therefore, in most instances, the clinician is actually working with a couple who is already involved in a pathogenic relationship rather than one that is merely at relationship risk.

Given the previous data, it is not surprising that there is increasing interest in the area of primary prevention. Primary prevention circumvents the difficulties of predicting individually at-risk couples (i.e., secondary prevention). Moreover, tertiary prevention amounts to treatment. The couple is already distressed, and professional intervention therefore functionally serves to limit the degree of marital pathology. Although the behavioral-communications model is clearly tertiary in nature, the therapeutic strategies included herein can be easily adapted for use in a primary prevention program. The rationale that underlies such primary prevention efforts is based upon the assumption that early intervention decreases the likelihood of later relational problems.

Markman, Floyd, and Dickson-Markman (1984) discuss three approaches to preventing marital distress: (a) premarital intervention, (b) marital/family enrichment programs, and (c) family skill training programs. All of these have been used to enhance couples' relationships and improve dyadic functioning, thereby reducing and/or preventing future marital distress. Premarital intervention programs usually incorporate one or more of the following components: (a) education (Rutledge, 1966), (b) enrichment (Mace, 1972), (c) nonspecific communication enhancement (Miller et al., 1975), (d) skill acquisition, and (e) cognitive restructuring (Markman & Floyd, 1980). Marital/family enrichment programs often focus on increasing the quality of couples' interactions and expanding awareness of each partner's needs. Although the content of these programs may vary, most emphasize communication skills (Otto, 1976) and are designed to "inoculate" participants against future relationship difficulties. Family skill training (Alexander, 1973) focuses upon the identification of coping skills within a family system and then behaviorally trains individuals to more effectively utilize these abilities. Although the targeted populations may differ, each of these approaches uses a mixture of components highly comparable to our earlier discussed principles of relationship change (see Chapter 2). We will now demonstrate how the primary elements of a behavioral-communications model have applicability within prevention-based programs.

## Preventive Aspects of the Behavioral-Communications Model

For didactic purposes, we will discuss prevention within six major areas: (a) understanding behavior, (b) objectification, (c) behavioral exchange, (d) compromise, (e) communications, and (f) problem-solving training.

*Understanding Behavior.* As previously discussed within the behavioral-communications model, behavior may serve two purposes: (a) behavior may literally be behavior (i.e., an expression of individual functioning), or (b) behavior may have relational value (i.e., has meaning within the relationship). In preventive programs, couples must learn to understand behavior in its relational sense, examining both their own and their partner's behaviors within an interactional framework. Thus, they may begin asking themselves any of the following questions:

1. What effect does my behavior have upon my partner?
2. What effect does my partner's behavior have upon me?
3. When I do "A," my partner responds by doing "B." Is that the result I would like to achieve?
4. When my partner does "C," I typically respond by doing "D." Are there other alternatives available to me?
5. If I were to do "E," what is my partner likely to do in response?
6. If my partner were to do "F," what am I likely to do in response?

Once a couple learns to understand behavior within its relational context, they can then "check out" and discuss issues in a more open and cooperative manner. Herein lies the essence of prevention—dealing with matters before they become problems.

*Objectification.* This process teaches the couple how to turn vague, global, and generalized statements of relationship satisfaction into well-specified descriptions of pleasing and displeasing behavior. Thus, a couple mastering this skill can learn to restructure nonfacilitative verbal messages into constructive information for relationship enhancement purposes. Incorporating objectification into primary prevention programs would appear to present no problem whatsoever. In fact, it has already been done (Alexander, 1973).

*Behavioral Exchange.* As we discussed earlier, reciprocity and behavioral exchange are conceptual and practical principles within the behavioral-communications treatment model. Quite simply, in both remedial and preventive programs, partners must learn to please one another. When individuals provide each other with positive behaviors, they are reinforced by their partner's appreciation and his/her reciprocal giving. Mutually rewarding behaviors increase, and the probability of marital success is substantially heightened. Consequently, behavioral exchange has clear and compelling utility within a prevention-based program.

*Compromise.* Behavioral-communications marital therapy experientially teaches partners a "give-to-get" principle; that is, "in order to get what I want, I must give some to my partner." Certainly, this notion forms the cornerstone of conflict resolution and problem-solving prevention programs. Those couples capable of using such skills have the means to effectively short-circuit problems before they arise.

*Communications.* Of all elements within the behavioral-communications model, communications probably serves the most psychoprophylactic function. Effective communications skills are essential to the attainment and maintenance of satisfying marital relations. Thus, it is not surprising that communications training is already a part of current prevention programs (Miller et al., 1975).

*Problem-solving Training.* As we have previously indicated, conflict is a natural by-product of long-term, intimate relationships. However, via problem-solving training, couples can learn equitable means of resolving their differences. Moreover, once learned, the problem-solving process can be applied across a wide variety of potentially destructive situations, thereby transforming conflict into cooperation. Once again, the preventive value is wholly apparent.

In sum, the behavioral-communications components just presented appear entirely congruent with prevention-based efforts. By instructing couples in effective relationship skills, one may be pragmatically curing the ills before the symptoms arise. This may be the direction that all marital therapists soon choose to pursue.

## SUMMARY

The behavioral-communications treatment approach places considerable emphasis on the maintenance and transfer of improved couples' interactions over time and across settings. This is accomplished by incorporating into the program a variety of maintenance strategies and technical procedures known to enhance generalization. Five of these strategies/procedures were discussed: (a) behavioral traps, (b) fading of contingencies, (c) expanding stimulus control, (d) self-control, and (e) peer facilitators. Although mental health professionals have generally shown little interest in prevention, increasing attention has been recently devoted to the topic. Following an outline of the classical prevention subdivisions, this chapter demonstrated a means by which behavioral-communications principles can be easily integrated into a prevention-based program. Thus, prevention was discussed within each of the following areas: (a) understanding behavior, (b) objectification, (c) behavioral exchange, (d) compromise, (e) communications, and (f) problem-solving training.

# Chapter 8
# Extended Case Examples

In this chapter, we will present three separate cases, each of which individually demonstrates different aspects of behavioral-communications marital therapy. In Case #1, considerable emphasis is placed on the integration of assessment and treatment aspects of the model. In Case #2, extensive detail is provided with respect to the intake interview. Case #3 deals with an extremely difficult couple who appear to resist virtually every therapeutic endeavor. In each of these instances, the reader is provided with an overview of the comprehensive treatment program. Moreover, examples of edited dialogue and specific treatment techniques are illustrated whenever possible. In addition, where appropriate, some commentary is provided with respect to the client, the therapist, or the strategy being exemplified.

## CASE #1: STEVE AND ELAINE W.

Mr. and Mrs. W. were referred for treatment by their family physician. Steve and Elaine had been married for 8 years and were childless. Steve, age 30, was self-employed in an automotive repair business, and Elaine, age 32, held a responsible clerical position in a locally based unit of the federal government. During the initial intake session, it became immediately apparent that Elaine was quite capable of voicing her dissatisfaction with the relationship. Steve, on the other hand, appeared rather unassertive, somber, and relatively nonverbal. Moreover, his repeated inability to effectively deal with relationship-based problems had only served to exacerbate Elaine's sense of frustration with the marriage. At the time of referral, the couple was in the process of considering separation, but no immediate action had yet been taken in that regard.

## Assessment

Three hour-long assessment sessions were conducted over a 3-week period of time. In addition to conjoint clinical interviews, a multidimensional assessment strategy was employed. This included use of the Locke-Wallace Marital Adjustment Test (MAT; Locke & Wallace, 1959), a modified version of the Marital Happiness Scale (MHS; Azrin et al., 1973), and a videotaped laboratory assessment. The MAT provided a pre-, post-, and follow-up measure of partners' self-reported marital satisfaction. The MHS provided information with respect to individual's rated happiness as a function of their spouse's behavior across 11 areas of common marital concern (maximum score = 110). This instrument was administered across all assessment and treatment sessions and thus served as a weekly, continuous measure of marital happiness within specified relationship dimensions. The videotaped laboratory assessment was a bit more complex than either of the previous two measures. During the laboratory assessment, Steve and Elaine engaged in videotaped discussions of marital problem situations. These situations were generated using a variation of Strodtbeck's (1951) Revealed Differences Technique. In this particular instance, Steve and Elaine had read a series of brief vignettes describing problematic marital situations that had been adapted from the Inventory of Marital Conflicts (Olson & Ryder, 1970). Independently, each spouse had been asked to indicate which individual within the vignette was responsible for the disagreement between partners. At the close of each assessment and treatment session, the couple was requested to role-play one randomly selected vignette about which they had disagreed. On each occasion, they were given 10 minutes to discuss and attempt to resolve their conflicts. Based upon the couple's complaints and retrospective ratings of the three assessment videotapes, four major target behaviors were then selected for the communications phase of treatment.

These role-play vignettes were rated by two judges using a modification of the Marital Interaction Coding System, (MICS; Marital Studies Center, 1975) and the Couples Interactional Scoring System (CISS; Gottman et al., 1977). The target behaviors selected for Steve and Elaine were complain, sidetracking, compromise, and humor. These were defined as follows.

*Complain.* This behavior was coded in those situations where the individual bemoans the extent of his/her suffering without explicitly blaming his/her spouse for such suffering ("I'm sick and tired of being poor"); statement must be delivered in an irritated tone of voice.

*Sidetracking.* This indicates any comment reflecting inability to remain on-task during a problem-solving discussion; scored when the client simply did not attend to spouse's remark or attempted to bring up an irrelevant topic of conversation (i.e., *Wife:* "We're $500 in debt this month already"; *Husband:* "Yeah, but I was thinking maybe we should go to the movies together tonight").

*Compromise.* This is a specific type of problem-solving behavior that culminates in the negotiation of a mutually acceptable behavioral exchange when partners were previously unable to resolve their differences.

*Humor.* This is any statement clearly intended to be funny, usually evoking laughter from the recipient (i.e., "When we get to the movie theater, let's walk in backwards, and if they ask what we're doing, we'll just tell them we're leaving!").

## Treatment

Marital therapy with Steve and Elaine went quite according to plan. During the first four sessions, primary emphasis was placed on increasing positive forms of interaction and developing more effective communications skills. Thus, at the close of the assessment period and prior to beginning therapy, Steve and Elaine was asked to complete a reciprocity awareness procedure (Azrin et al., 1973). This involved both partners receiving the following assignment:

> *Therapist:* I would like both of you to create a list of positive and negative partner behaviors—that is, the things that your partner does that you find satisfying and those things that he/she does that are somewhat objectionable. I want you to do that independently of one another and then bring those lists with you when you come in for our next meeting. Do you have any questions?

Both partners brought the lists with them to the first session and under the therapist's direction began behaviorally specifying what they really appreciated about one another. An excerpt of this interaction is presented below:

> *Elaine: (to Steve)* You're a kind person, and that's something I really think is unique about you.
> *Steve: (nods head)*
> *Therapist:* Elaine, can you be more specific for Steve? What is it that makes him kind? What does he do that allows you to conclude he's a kind person?
> *Elaine:* Well, he's different than other men. . . .
> *Therapist:* No, I want you to tell him directly. Talk to Steve, not to me.
> *Elaine:* Okay, you're different than most other men, or at least different than how I think most other men are. You're soft-spoken and sincere. You may not always have a lot to say, but when you do say something it's usually kind and gentle. I really don't think you would ever go out of your way to hurt anyone or anything.
> *Steve:* Hmm, I don't know what to say. I mean, I don't know what to say right now.

*Therapist:* (*to Steve*) That's okay. (*to Elaine*) That was very good, but I wonder if you could give Steve a recent example of a situation where you saw him being kind as you just spoke about it.

*Elaine:* Yeah, I think so. Last week when my mom called to tell us about my Aunt Audrey's illness, you were really nice. I mean, you hardly even know my aunt. She's never had very much to do with us at all, but my mom was obviously upset and I thought you were really wonderful with her. You listened, you told her everything would probably be all right, you calmed her down—you were just amazingly giving. That's something that I really appreciate about you. (*eyes beginning to fill with tears*)

*Steve:* She's your mother. Of course, I'm going to listen and try to help. I care about her.

*Therapist:* (*to Elaine*) And it looks like you care about Steve—that there are some things that he does that really make you feel very good.

*Elaine:* God, yes. That's why I get so upset when I see him do some of these other things that just drive me crazy.

*Therapist:* Hold it! Remember, right now we're talking about the things you appreciate. We'll get to the other side of the list, but we're not quite ready for that right now. Let's go back. Tell Steve directly that the kindness is something that you really appreciate.

*Elaine:* Okay, like I said, when you do that kind of thing with my mom, I just feel so good about you. I know we've got our problems and that's why we're here, but that kind of thing, the kindness and the niceness, is so special . . . (*hesitatingly*) it really is. (*teary*)

*Therapist:* (*to Steve*) How does it feel to hear that kind of thing from Elaine?

*Steve:* It really feels good. We don't say those kind of things to one another or, if we do, I guess we don't always hear them.

*Therapist:* Yes, but when you do say them or your partner hears them it sure makes a difference, doesn't it?

*Steve:* Sure does. (*reaches over, holds Elaine's hand, and speaks to her*) Thank you.

As is, it is hoped, apparent from the previous transcript, this was a rather moving encounter. Obviously, up until this point much of Elaine's and Steve's interaction had been in the pattern of demanding–withdrawal–hostile–withdrawal. By simply focusing on some of the reasons why they appreciated each other in the first place, they were once again reminded of what it was that they truly valued in each other. This had enormously positive consequences in therapy. It appeared as though a mutual respect and sense of trust had been infused into the relationship. The therapist's job, however, was to maintain this good feeling while simultaneously increasing communications skills and resolving particular areas of dispute within the relationship. One of the ways in which this was accomplished was via a "caring days-refusal" procedure. Using this technique, individuals made a listing of partner generated behaviors that would increase their satisfaction in the relationship. However, because assertiveness appeared to be an issue for Steve in particular, some emphasis was placed upon the "refusal" component of the program. An excerpt from session three is provided:

> *Therapist:* I notice on Elaine's caring days list of last week that there's one behavior that never happened at all—"tell me what checks you've written." What's that all about?
>
> *Elaine:* Well, if I don't know what checks Steve has written, I don't know how much money there is in the account, and then we might end up overdrawing the balance.
>
> *Therapist:* (*to Elaine*) So that didn't happen last week? I mean, Steve didn't inform you of the checks he had written? Is that right?
>
> *Elaine:* Right. (*to Steve*) You didn't, did you?
>
> *Steve:* No, I don't think so.
>
> *Therapist:* (*thinking to self: "I wonder what this is all about?"*) (*to Steve*) I get the impression that's difficult for you—that you really don't like reporting to Elaine about your checks. What do you think?
>
> *Steve:* Kind of . . . I don't know, I'm not sure.
>
> *Therapist:* Okay, let's see if I can help. Steve, you come over here and take my chair, and I'll move over into your chair for a minute. (*to Elaine*) I'm going to be Steve for a minute here. Let's see (*thinking*). Elaine, I think I've got a problem with this one caring days item related to the checking account.
>
> *Elaine:* Yeah, what's that?
>
> *Therapist:* Well, I'm not sure, but it kind of feels like when I'm reporting to you what checks I've written that you're sort of looking over my shoulder approving or disapproving of what I've done, and that doesn't feel good to me.
>
> *Elaine:* What else can I do? We need to balance our checkbooks, don't we?
>
> *Therapist:* Oh, I'm not disagreeing with that. I'm just saying that coming in and reporting to you what checks I've written makes me feel like a little kid telling his mom how many failing grades he got. (*to Steve*) Is that pretty close?
>
> *Steve:* It sure is!
>
> *Elaine:* (*to Steve*) Okay, I can understand how you feel, but what can we do about it?
>
> *Therapist:* Hold on. First, Steve, why don't you come back over here and I'll get back into my own chair. (*therapist and Steve switch chairs*) Now, let's decide if we want that item to stay on Elaine's caring days list. Steve, what do you think?
>
> *Steve:* I guess I'd feel most comfortable if we could get rid of it.
>
> *Therapist:* Tell that to Elaine.
>
> *Steve:* Right. Well, like we've already said, it does make me feel kind of uncomfortable reporting to you about checks. I'd feel best if we deleted that item from your list and added something in its place.
>
> *Elaine:* Okay with me, but how do we then balance the checkbooks?
>
> *Therapist:* Slow down. Remember, in here we do things one step at a time. First, we decide if it's to be deleted. Then, what goes in its place. And after that, how we deal with the issue of balancing the checkbook. Okay? Let's go back to step one. Are you two in agreement that it should be deleted because Steve doesn't feel very good about it?
>
> *Elaine/Steve:* Yes.

The reader will want to note several things about this selected interchange. First, "caring days-refusal" procedures are appropriate for most couples, but they are especially appropriate for this couple, given Steve's general inability to assert himself. Second, the use of therapist modeling clearly gave Steve permission to openly express his feelings about Elaine's caring days request. Third, the therapist took control and obviously slowed down the process, placing emphasis on those elements that were most apt to facilitate the process of change. Fourth, the therapist's closing comment clearly indicates that the couple was about to embark on the problem-solving enterprise (i.e., how to balance the checkbook). In point of fact, this is exactly what occurred over the course of sessions four through seven. Each of these sessions was spaced at 2-week intervals with the seventh session occurring 3 weeks later. Some of the problem-solving issues confronted during these sessions included: (a) Steve's career goals, (b) responsibility for decision-making, (c) raising a family, and (d) positive coupling activities. In all instances, Steve and Elaine were able to reach mutually acceptable resolution to their differences. Moreover, although the therapist remained moderately active throughout the treatment phase, less structured interventions were required over time. Indeed, during the eighth and final session (scheduled 1 month after the seventh session), the therapist made very limited verbal interventions, because Steve and Elaine spent most of the hour enjoyably discussing their recent attempts at conceiving a child and how they could best prepare for and deal with future conflict when it arose.

## Results

In addition to the pre-, post-, and continuous assessments, Steve and Elaine were contacted 1 year following their initial referral. At that time, a brief interview was held, and all measures were once again readministered. The results of their assessment for MAT and MHS data are indicated in Table 8.1. The laboratory-based observations are presented in Figure 8.1. These rate per minute data indicate clear and dramatic improvement for all target behaviors. Moreover, observations conducted during the follow-up probe reveal a rather consistent pattern of maintenance over time. In sum, all evidence indicates a highly successful therapeutic endeavor.

## CASE #2: JON AND MORA L.

Jon and Mora had been married for 9 years at the time of referral. Jon, age 35, was a school teacher and active political figure in the community. Mora, age 33, was a full-time student at the university majoring in soci-

Table 8.1. Steve and Elaine's Assessment
at Pre-, Post-, and Follow-up

|           | MAT | | MHS | |
|-----------|-------|--------|-------|--------|
|           | Steve | Elaine | Steve | Elaine |
| Pre-      | 90    | 73     | 70    | 58     |
| Post-     | 107   | 110    | 75    | 87     |
| Follow-up | 110   | 113    | 90    | 97     |

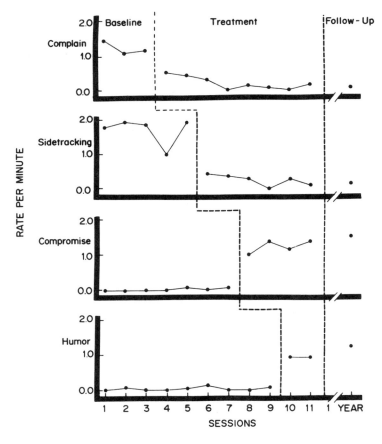

FIGURE 8.1. Laboratory Data Across Baseline, Treatment, and Follow-up Phases

ology and social work. The Ls appeared for therapy indicating that their relationship had lost its "energy." Upon questioning, it became clear that, while enthusiasm and vitality had drained from the relationship over time, Jon had also been involved with another woman. The Ls had one child, Rebecca, age 5 years.

As a demonstration of behavioral-communications marital therapy, there are a number of aspects of this case that are quite interesting. Let us begin by examining a portion of the intake interview.

## Intake Interview

*Therapist:* What is it that brings you folks in?

*Jon:* We've had some rough times lately. It seems as though we don't spend very much time together, and when we do, things don't always go that well.

*Mora:* Well, I think it's even more than that. Jon never seems really happy anymore. He works very hard, he has lots of responsibility, but when he comes home we don't seem to be able to relax and enjoy each other the way we used to.

*Jon:* Yeah, I agree. We're not together that much, and when we are it's sort of like two ships passing in the night. You know, she's there and I'm there, but not much else is happening.

*Therapist:* So part of the problem is an *absence* of positive things happening between you two?

*Jon:* Definitely.

*Mora:* Yes but . . . it's more than that.

*Therapist:* More than that?

*Mora:* Yeah, Jon sort of formed a friendship with another teacher at his school last year, and that's caused some hard feeling between us.

*Therapist:* Uh, huh. Just what kind of friendship was this?

*Jon:* Well, I might as well be honest about it. This woman is a teacher in my school and she and her husband were having some pretty serious problems. He's an alcoholic and was just abusing the hell out of her. Well, to make a long story short, she talked to me about it, and I told her exactly what I thought—she didn't need that idiot and she certainly didn't deserve that kind of treatment. Anyhow, it didn't take her very long to recognize that, and she ended up leaving him, and I think they actually got divorced sometime last month.

*Mora:* You don't think they got divorced sometime last month. You know they got divorced last month.

*Therapist:* (*to Jon*) So this relationship between you and the woman has continued for some time?

*Jon:* Yeah, sort of.

*Therapist:* (*to Jon and Mora*) What is this "sort of" stuff? Either it has or it hasn't. Which is it?

*Jon:* It has.

*Therapist:* And it's still continuing now?

*Jon:* Yeah, but it's not what Mora thinks.

*Mora:* I don't know what to think.

*Therapist:* Actually, that's fine because I'm getting the impression that you two haven't actually discussed this whole thing real openly. Is that right?

*Mora:* Well, we've discussed it, but, like I said, I'm not sure exactly what's gone on in the past and what's going on right now.

*Jon:* Like I've told you before, it's not that serious. She was in a bad situation, I've helped her out and given her some support. Yeah, we got a little involved but nothing . . . extreme. I mean, I'm not about to leave you and Rebecca and run off to Tahiti with Nancy.

*Therapist:* I don't think the issue is Tahiti right now. I think the issue is whether this relationship with Nancy is going to continue, *in any form,* while we're trying to work on the relationship between you two. (*pointing to Jon and Mora*)

*Jon:* I don't understand.

*Therapist:* Then let me make myself perfectly clear. If you're going to work with me on your (*again, pointing to Jon and Mora*) relationship, then I will insist that we do just that. I cannot be of service to you two if there is a third party somewhere in the background. Therefore, while we are finding out whether your marriage is going to make it or not in here, I must ask that you put all other relationships "on hold." In essence, such relationships must end, at least for the time being, while we explore this one. That goes for both of you.

*Mora:* I understand that.

*Jon:* I guess I still don't understand. I mean I work with this other woman. I see her everyday. What am I supposed to do about that? When she comes up to me in the hall and starts a conversation, am I supposed to say nothing, turn, and walk away?

*Therapist:* I guess what you say at that particular point in time is entirely up to you. All I'm saying is that what we do in here is work. It takes time and energy. If any of your energies are devoted to some kind of an involvement outside of this relationship, it won't work. I don't mean the marriage won't work, I mean what we're trying to do won't work. We're trying to find out if you guys can make it together—I am not committed to your making it or not making it, one way or the other, but I am committed to aiding you in finding out what's in your best interests and where you go from here. Quite frankly, that's no easy job, and if we're going to give it a try, we're going to have to work at it on a full-time basis. No third-party relationships—that's my bottom line, at least for now. What you two decide for later is entirely up to you, but that's what I decided for now. Is that clear?

*Jon/Mora:* Yeah.

*Therapist:* Okay, this obviously is going to take a little thought on your part. I'd therefore like to ask the following. I'd like you two to go home and think some about what we've said today. Then, I'd like you to discuss it and reach some kind of a joint decision as to whether we want to give this a try or not. In either case, I'd like a phone call from you informing me of your decision by a week from today. If you decide no, that's fine. If you decide yes, then we'll set up our next appointment when we speak on the phone. I will also have an assignment ready for you at that time, so when we talk I'd like to be able to talk to you both at the same time. Do you have an extension phone at home?

*Jon/Mora:* Yes.

*Therapist:* Okay. Then, when you call, or if I call you back, I'll ask that you're both on the phone so that we can all talk together. All right, do you have any questions for me?

*Jon:* I don't think so.

*Mora:* Nope.

*Therapist:* Very good. Thanks for coming in today, and I look forward to hearing from you soon.

There are a number of aspects of this intake session that bear further comment. First, the therapist has obviously taken a very hard line with respect to continuing the third-party relationship. Without belaboring that issue, it certainly appeared to be a major stumbling block to effective therapy. Both Jon and Mora were involved in a mutual denial of the extramarital affair. Thus, Jon's involvement with Nancy needed to be confronted but not explicitly. Had the therapist pursued the sordid details of that relationship during the first session, we doubt that the couple could have dealt with the information in any positive way. Second, the therapist refused to engage in Jon's manipulative game when he asked what to do about Nancy. To have answered his question specifically would only have furthered the couple's communication pattern that already existed. That is, Jon could then continue to violate the spirit, if not the letter of the law. Thus, by simply reiterating the demand of no third-party relationships, the therapist disengaged from the petty question and focused instead on the more overriding issue (i.e., "Are you going to continue to be involved with her or not?"). Third, clearly the therapist took control of the interaction, both literally and figuratively. Literally, the therapist had quite a bit to say. This information truly needed to be presented, though. Figuratively, the message was all important: "I know what I'm doing, and I have no bias with respect to making your marriage work or not." Lastly, the therapist was concerned that Jon may have felt attacked or unsupported. This was a real risk, and one that was confronted immediately in therapy.

## Treatment

Jon and Mora telephoned the therapist and indicated they were willing to continue in treatment. One further assessment session was held, at which time the clinical interview was completed and psychometric instruments administered (i.e., MSTL, DAS, MSI, and SOC). The results of this assessment indicated: (a) a limited amount of time together, (b) considerable global distress within the relationship, (c) numerous areas of conflict/discord, and (d) a low P : D ratio. As a consequence, a treatment program designed to remedy these problems was immediately put into effect. For example, the initial telephone homework assignment asked both Jon and Mora to objectify their partner's strengths and weaknesses in the relationship. Table 8.2 presents this information. After their training in behavioral specification, a number of relationship matters became quite clear. First, Jon and Mora still liked and respected one another. Second, their schedules were so overcommitted that they virtually had no time to be together. Third, the number of pleasing activities that they jointly shared was dismally low. Fourth, they were not presently communicating with each other in an effective manner. Their mutual respect and admiration was promoted by focusing the initial therapy session upon the relationship strengths. Overcommitment in scheduling was later confronted by having Jon and Mora prioritize their responsibilities. Subsequently, they initiated a "quality time" program where they set aside time just for themselves as a couple. Further, the number of pleasing activities was increased via the use of the "cookie jar" technique (Weiss & Birchler, 1978). Here, both individuals made a list of pleasing activities that their partner could initiate on their behalf. These were written on folded slips of paper and placed in an appropriately labeled cookie jar ("his" and "hers"). Each partner committed himself/herself to randomly drawing and acting upon a number of these requests on a weekly basis. Jon and Mora seemed to enjoy the game-like quality of this behavioral exchange procedure, and

Table 8.2. Partners' Strengths and Weaknesses in the Relationship

| Jon's Strengths | Mora's Strengths |
| --- | --- |
| Friendly to almost anyone | Can listen intently |
| Enthusiastic | Very kind—empathizes |
| Follows through on commitment | Likes sports |
| Generous | Serious and intense |
| Kind and considerate sex partner | Knows how to look nice |
| Neat | Has many friends |
| Has a way with people | Smiles a lot |
| Has a calming effect on me | Likes humor—as teller or listener |
| Good sense of humor | Always gains success whenever she goes |
| Likes to have a good time | for it |
| Shows his emotions | Has had much patience with me |
| Makes people feel good | Great in morning |
|  | Helps me with writing |

| Jon's Weaknesses | Mora's Weaknesses |
| --- | --- |
| Not enough time for family | Too busy |
| Defensive | Getting a little flabby |
| Takes things too personally | Stays at home too much |
| Argumentative (especially when drunk) | Sexually conservative |
| Unrealistic expectations of me | Doesn't know her own potential |
| Too independent—doesn't ask for my | Goes overboard with animals |
| help often enough |  |
| Nancy |  |

the positive results achieved were immediately apparent in their relationship. Lastly, communication and problem-solving were improved as a result of the behavioral-communications training program. An example of its application with Jon and Mora is presented below:

> *Jon:* One of the things that's upsetting to me is that we seem to get stuck in ruts all too easily.
> *Therapist:* (*to Mora*) Do you understand what he means?
> *Mora:* No, not really.
> *Therapist:* Then ask him to explain it better.
> *Mora:* Okay. What do you mean stuck in ruts?
> *Jon:* You know, we tend to do the same things all the time. Not a whole lot new seems to happen to us. It's all very regular and predictable.
> *Mora:* And boring?
> *Jon:* Kind of. I don't mean to sound critical, it's just that when things are that predictable, it is a little boring.
> *Therapist:* (*to Jon*) And you'd like a little more excitement, a little more pizzazz in the relationship. Right?
> *Jon:* Yeah, I think so.
> *Mora:* I've got no problem with that as long as we still take care of our responsibilities. I mean, I assume you're not asking me to let Nancy move in with us.
> *Jon:* Don't be ridiculous—of course not.
> *Therapist:* Well, how can you two put a little more excitement back in the relationship?
> *Mora:* I don't know.
> *Jon:* I think we've already started, but I guess I'd like to make sure we continue with it and maybe even make it stronger.
> *Therapist:* (*to Jon*) I get the impression you have some things in mind.
> *Jon:* Well, maybe a few things.
> *Therapist:* Great. Why don't you tell Mora directly and let's see what she thinks. Go ahead.
> *Jon:* Okay. Well, first I think we could jazz up our sex life a little bit. . . .

This interaction was fairly representative of how Jon and Mora began dealing with issues just as this. In fact, the issue of excitement led directly to a later discussion of Jon's former relationship with Nancy. What became clear was that Jon was never really very interested in Nancy per se, but rather simply found himself becoming more and more dissatisfied with the boredom and predictability of his marriage. Obviously, some of this predictability was both healthy and necessary in the relationship. On the other hand, too much created a conventionality that was doing considerably more harm than good.

## Results

Jon and Mora were seen for a total of 12 sessions. The first six sessions were held at weekly intervals, the following four sessions at biweekly intervals, and the final two sessions 1 month apart. Continuous and pre–post measures indicated improvement across all areas of the relationship that had been assessed. Furthermore, a follow-up client satisfaction questionnaire (Larsen et al., 1979) indicated an extremely positive reaction to the entire program. Overall, our global evaluation of this particular couple would indicate that the treatment was extremely successful.

## CASE #3: DON AND ERIN R.

Don and Erin R. had been married for 12 years at the time of referral. Don, age 38, was an attorney in private practice. Erin, age 36, was a homemaker and part-time secretary for a local large employer in the community. The couple was self-referred, complaining of a number of very serious relationship problems. Erin was extremely upset with her role as homemaker and clearly blamed Don for always placing her in a "one-down" position. Moreover, she felt that he lacked understanding and sensitivity to her needs. Don, on the other hand, indicated that as far as Erin was concerned he could "do no right." In addition, he was tired of trying to please her when basically she was "unpleaseable." Whenever Don and Erin attempted to communicate about problems in the relationship, one of two things would happen: They would either argue loudly and angrily, or one partner would attack, and the other would refuse to talk entirely. This general state of affairs had apparently been in existence for quite some time but had sorely deteriorated over the past 2 years. The R's had two children: a son, Jason, age 10 years, and a daughter, Tamara, age 8 years.

### Assessment and Treatment

Two sessions of assessment were conducted, comprised of paper-and-pencil instruments as well as direct observation of the couple's problem-solving behavior. These results did not bode well. Findings revealed tremendous dissatisfaction with the relationship, a wide variety of conflict areas (e.g., finances, household responsibilities, independence, consideration, etc.), limited positive interaction, and a highly pathological communications process. For example, when the couple was given the opportunity to discuss ways in which they might generate more pleasing behaviors for one another, notice how the deterioration rapidly occurs:

> *Therapist:* All right, Don says he would be willing to do some things around the house that would relieve some of your responsibility, Erin. Now, why don't you tell him specifically what he could do?
> *Erin:* He can shove it!
> *Therapist:* What?
> *Erin:* That's right, he can shove it! Why all of a sudden is he willing to help out? I'll tell you why. Because he doesn't want to look like the son-of-a-bitch he is in front of you. Sure, he'll help, but only . . .

*Therapist: (interrupts, to Erin)* Wait a second. I realize that you're angry and real distrustful of Don right now, and I'm sure you feel as though you've got good reason for that, but the fact of the matter is that he has said he's willing to try to change some things. Why don't we work with that right now? Okay?

*Erin:* I've been here before but, sure, let's try. *(sarcastically)*

*Therapist: (to Erin)* Okay, once again, then, what could he do that would be of some help around the house?

*Erin:* You know, I have to admit this bothers me.

*Therapist: (to Erin)* What's that?

*Erin:* Well, here we sit acting as if Don doesn't know what he could do around the house. What a crock! He knows exactly what he could do if he really wanted to help. The fact is, he doesn't want to help—he doesn't care. All he cares about is himself.

*Don: (to therapist)* You see what I have to put up with? *(to Erin)* You're a shrew; a nagging, unforgiving bitch! I've never. . . .

*Therapist: (interrupting)* Hold it! You're going nowhere folks. You want to fight and name-call, go right ahead and do it, but not on my time. I'm going up front by the main desk—when you're finished arguing, come on up and get me. I'll be waiting there for you. *(therapist leaves)*

The previous sequence of events is highly representative of this couple's normal interaction. The therapist was forced to constantly interrupt and attempt to redirect their communication. Unfortunately, it seemed that virtually all interventions failed or had only limited degrees of effectiveness. In fact, assuming that the couple needed to learn to control their vengeful arguing, the therapist even attempted to paradoxically assign homework in this area (Wilson & Bornstein, 1984). Consequently, arguing was positively reframed as a means by which they could uncover their real differences. Furthermore, Don and Erin were told to go home and argue for one-half hour each night as ferociously as they could (Weeks & L'Abate, 1982). Although this particular tactic did seem to have some limited success (i.e., they argued on only one-third of the available occasions), it certainly did not advance any positive forms of interaction between them. Indeed, after four sessions of repeated therapeutic impotence, the following exchange took place:

*Therapist:* You know, I get the distinct impression that you folks are more interested in arguing and hurting one another than actually trying to change your situation in any kind of positive manner. That's not meant as a criticism, that's meant as a factual statement about what seems to be going on in here. I wonder what your reaction to that is?

*Don:* I think you're probably right. It certainly does seem to be the case.

*Erin:* Why shouldn't it be the case? Maybe we've been hurt for so long that all we want to do is get back at the other guy.

*Therapist:* Why don't you take responsibility for that statement—"I've been hurt for so long. . . . "

*Erin:* Well, it's true. I have been hurt for so long and I'm not about to get hurt by you [Don] again.

*Don:* I really can't imagine what I've done that makes you so contemptuous of me.

*Erin:* That's the saddest part of all. You don't even know what a poor excuse for a husband you are.

*Therapist:* Here we go again. *(to Erin)* Instead of attacking right now, why don't you try explaining to Don what he's done in the past and continues to do today that's so upsetting? I think that would be more helpful.

*Erin:* Nothing would be helpful. I've explained it a hundred times. I'm out of energy for explaining it again. If he doesn't know by now, that's too goddamn bad.

*Therapist:* Okay. *(to Don)* She's made it perfectly clear. Erin is giving up. She finds the situation hopeless. As far as she is concerned, things cannot improve. *(to Erin)* That's right, isn't it?

*Erin:* Yup.

*Therapist:* Well, Don, where does that leave you?

*Don:* I'm not exactly sure. I mean this whole thing is a mess, but I'm not sure what to do with it. I'm really at a loss.

*Therapist:* Well, I'm not. I think the handwriting is on the wall. You folks have had your fill of each other. There's really not much left except a lot of bad feeling. Maybe it's time you packed up shop and called it quits.

*Erin:* *(tearful)* What about Jason and Tamara?

*Therapist:* What about them? They won't be the first kids to have divorced parents. Plus, do you really think they don't know what's going on?

*Erin:* I don't know; I just don't know.

*Therapist:* Well, for the first time since we started meeting, you two are finally in agreement—neither of you knows what to do. That's going to be your assignment for this week. Now that we know just how deep the hurt is and that the situation is considered just about hopeless by both of you, where do we go from here? In other words, I want you two to talk about just exactly what options exist for you at this point in time. Then, when we get together next week, I'd like to look at the list of options that you've come up with and see if we can't narrow them down some. Okay.

*Don/Erin:* Okay.

This is your basic "calling a spade a spade" therapy. The relationship really could not be much worse. These people were in agony living with one another. After the therapist had explored a wide range of therapeutic interventions and seen them all fail, it simply seemed most appropriate to take them to the brink of divorce and see what they did with it. The results were interesting. Three days later, the therapist received a phone call from Erin stating that they had decided that divorce was both extreme and perhaps premature, and that instead they had decided to stay together and work things out by themselves. The therapist indicated that, although the decision was theirs to make, it would certainly be wise to examine it more fully with everyone present and strongly recommended that this be discussed at the next scheduled session. The therapist also indicated, as had been explained earlier, that the nature of the phone conversation would probably be discussed in that meeting as well. Erin said that would be fine, and arrangements were made to meet the following week. On the day of the appointed meeting, Don called in and left the following message: "Things going well. We'll give it a try on our own. Thanks for your help. Don and Erin R."

The therapist did manage to recontact them by telephone and speak to both of them at the same time. That conversation did not provide much information at all, and the R's were insistent that they would not come in for even a one-time follow-up session. Our best guess is actually quite simple. The R's did not want to change the nature of their relationship. They were actually quite satisfied with their embattled, aggressive posture. It would appear that the relationship in its present form served a purpose. Namely, making life miserable for each other had a higher priority than working toward any real solution to the R's marital woes. When the therapist basically refused to allow the game to continue, the clients refused to continue in therapy. Therapy was therefore terminated at the clients' request after four sessions of treatment.

## SUMMARY

Three separate cases were presented as examples of behavioral-communications marital therapy. The first and second case examples provide illustrations of treatments that ran their full course and were generally evaluated as highly successful. The third case, on the other hand, provides overview of a treatment that appeared to be of limited utility and resulted in premature termination. In each case example, attempts were made to provide the reader with both assessment and treatment information. Moreover, transcripts of therapist-client dialogue and technological details of implementation allow for thorough examination of the overall therapeutic process.

# References

Albrecht, S. L. (1980). Reactions and adjustments to divorce: Differences in the experience of males and females. *Family Relations, 29,* 59–68.

Alexander, J. F. (1973). Defensive and supportive communication in normal and deviant families. *Journal of Consulting and Clinical Psychology, 40,* 223–231.

Alexander, J. F., Barton, C., Schiavo, R. S., & Parsons, B. V. (1976). Behavioral intervention with families of delinquents: Therapist characteristics and outcome. *Journal of Consulting and Clinical Psychology, 44,* 656–664.

Alexander, J. F., & Parsons, B. V. (1982). *Functional family therapy.* Monterey, CA: Brooks/Cole.

Atkeson, B. M., Forehand, R. L., & Rickard, K. M. (1982). The effects of divorce on children. In B. B. Lahey & A. E. Kazdin (Eds.), *Advances in clinical child psychology* (Vol. 5, pp. 255–281). New York: Plenum.

Azrin, N. H., Naster, B. J., & Jones, R. (1973). Reciprocity counseling: A rapid learning-based procedure for marital counseling. *Behaviour Research and Therapy, 11,* 365–382.

Baer, D. M., Rowbury, T. G., & Goetz, E. M. (1976). Behavioral types in the preschool: A proposal for research. *Minnesota Symposium on Child Psychology, 10,* 3–27.

Baer, D. M., & Wolf, M. M. (1970). The entry into natural communities of reinforcement. In R. Ulrich, T. Stachnik, & J. Mabry (Eds.), *Control of human behavior* (Vol. 2). Glenview, IL: Scott, Foresman.

Bandler, R., Grinder, J., & Satir, V. (1976). *Changing with families.* Palo Alto, CA: Science and Behavior Books.

Bandura, A. (1969). *Principles of behavior modification.* New York: Holt, Rinehart, & Winston.

Baucom, D. H. (1981). *Cognitive behavioral strategies in the treatment of marital discord.* Paper presented at the meeting of the Association for the Advancement of Behavior Therapy, Toronto, Canada.

Berg, P., & Snyder, D. K. (1981). Differential diagnosis of marital and sexual distress: A multidimensional approach. *Journal of Sex and Marital Therapy, 7,* 290–295.

Bienvenu, M. J. (1970). Measurement of marital communication. *The Family Coordinator, 19,* 26–31.

Birchler, G. R., Weiss, R. L., & Vincent, J. P. (1975). A multimethod analysis of social reinforcement exchange between maritally distressed and nondistressed spouse and stranger dyads. *Journal of Personality and Social Psychology, 31,* 349–360.

Bornstein, M. T. (1985). *Development and evaluation of a group-based program for children of divorce.* Unpublished master's thesis, University of Montana, Missoula, MT.

Bornstein, P. H., Anton, B., Harowski, K. J., Weltzien, R. T., McIntyre, T. J., & Hocker, J. (1981). Behavioral-communications treatment of marital discord: Positive behaviors. *Behavioral Counseling Quarterly, 1,* 189–201.

Bornstein, P. H., Bach, P. J., Heider, J. F., & Ernst, J. (1981). Clinical treatment of marital dysfunction: A multiple-baseline analysis. *Behavioral Assessment, 3,* 335–343.

Bornstein, P. H., Bornstein, M. T., & Dawson, B. (1984). Integrated assessment and treatment. In T. H. Ollendick & M. Hersen (Eds.), *Child behavioral assessment: Principles and procedures* (pp. 223–244). Elmsford, NY: Pergamon.

Bornstein, P. H., Fisher, D. C., & Balleweg, B. J. (1982). Problem-solving in couples: A guide for clinical research and applied practice. *Scandinavian Journal of Behaviour Therapy, 11,* 1–13.

Bornstein, P. H., Fox, S. G., Sturm, C. A., Balleweg, B. J., Kirby, K. L., Wilson, G. L., Weisser, C. E., Andre, J. C., & McLellarn, R. W. (1983). Treatment acceptability of alternative marital therapies: A comparative analysis. *Journal of Marital and Family Therapy, 9,* 205–208.

Bornstein, P. H., Hamilton, S. B., & Bornstein, M. T. (1985). Self-monitoring procedures. In A. R. Ciminero, K. S. Calhoun, & H. E. Adams (Eds.), *Handbook of behavioral assessment.* New York: Wiley.

Bornstein, P. H., Hickey, J. S., Schulein, M. J., Fox, S. G., & Scolatti, M. J. (1983). Behavioral communications treatment of marital interaction: Negative behaviors. *British Journal of Clinical Psychology, 22,* 41–48.

Bornstein, P. H., Kazdin, A. E., & McIntyre, T. J. (1985). Characteristics, trends, and future directions in child behavior therapy. In P. H. Bornstein & A. E. Kazdin (Eds.), *Handbook of clinical behavior therapy with children* (pp. 546–559). Homewood, IL: Dow Jones-Irwin.

Bornstein, P. H., & Quevillon, R. (1976). The effects of self-instructional package on overactive boys. *Journal of Applied Behavior Analysis, 9,* 179–188.

Bornstein, P. H., & Rychtarik, R. G. (1983). Consumer satisfaction in adult behavior therapy: Procedure, problems, and future perspectives. *Behavior Therapy, 14,* 191–208.

Bornstein, P. H., Wilson, G. L., Balleweg, B. J., Weisser, C. E., Bornstein, M. T., Andre, J. C., Woody, D. J., Smith, M. M., Laughna, S. M., McLellarn, R. W., Kirby, K. L., & Hocker, J. (1984). Behavioral marital bibiotherapy: An initial investigation of therapeutic efficacy. *The American Journal of Family Therapy, 12,* 21–28.

Bornstein, P. H., Wilson, G. L., Bornstein, M. T., Balleweg, B. J., Weisser, C. E., Andre, J. C., Smith, M. M., Woody, D. J., Laughna, S. M., McLellarn, R. W., Kirby, K. L., & Hocker, J. (1985). Behavioral cohabitation: Increasing satisfaction among non-married dyads? *Journal of Sex and Marital Therapy, 11,* 113–120.

Bundza, K. A., & Simonson, N. R. (1973). Therapist self-disclosure: Its effect on impressions of therapist and willingness to disclose. *Psychotherapy: Theory, Research and Practice, 10,* 215–217.

Carter, H., & Glick, P. C. (1976). *Marriage and divorce: A social and economic study.* Cambridge, MA: Harvard University Press.

Christensen, A., & Nies, D. C. (1980). The spouse observation checklist: Empirical analysis and critique. *The American Journal of Family Therapy, 8,* 69–79.

Cousins, P. C., & Vincent, J. P. (1983). Supportive and aversive behavior following spousal complaints. *Journal of Marriage and the Family, 45,* 679–682.

Crosby, J. F. (1985). *Illusion and disillusion: The self in love and marriage.* Belmont, CA: Wadsworth.

Cumming, E. (1972). Primary prevention—more cost than benefit. In H. Gottesfeld (Ed.), *The critical issues of community mental health.* New York: Behavioral Publications.

Davidson, B., Balswick, J., & Halverson, C. (1983). Affective self-disclosure and marital adjustment: A test of equity theory. *Journal of Marriage and the Family, 43,* 93–102.

Egan, G. (1975). *The skilled helper: A model for systematic helping and interpersonal relating.* Monterey, CA: Brooks/Cole.

Eidelson, R. J., & Epstein, N. (1982). Cognition and relationship maladjustment: Development of a measure of dysfunctional relationship beliefs. *Journal of Consulting and Clinical Psychology, 50,* 715–720.

Eisler, R. M., & Hersen, M. (1973). Behavioral techniques in family-oriented crisis intervention. *Archives of General Psychiatry, 28,* 111–116.

Ekman, P., & Friesen, W. V. (1969). Nonverbal leakage and cues to deception. *Psychiatry*, *32*, 88–105.

Ellis, A. (1962). *Reason and emotion in psychotherapy*. New York: Lyle Stuart.

Ely, A. L., Guerney, G. B., & Stover, L. (1973). Efficacy of the training phase of conjugal therapy. *Psychotherapy: Theory, Research and Practice*, *10*, 201–207.

Emshoff, J. G., Redd, W. H., & Davidson, W. S. (1976). Generalization training and the transfer of treatment effects with delinquent adolescents. *Journal of Behavior Therapy and Experimental Psychiatry*, *7*, 141–144.

Epstein, N. (1982). Cognitive therapy with couples. *American Journal of Family Therapy*, *10*, 5–16.

Epstein, N., & Eidelson, R. J. (1981). Unrealistic beliefs of clinical couples: Their relationship to expectations, goals and satisfaction. *American Journal of Family Therapy*, *9*, 13–22.

Felixbrod, J. J., & O'Leary, K. D. (1974). Self-determination of academic standards: Towards freedom from external control. *Journal of Educational Psychology*, *66*, 845–850.

Filsinger, E. E., & Lewis, R. A. (1981). *Assessing marriage: New behavioral approaches*. Beverly Hills, CA: Sage.

Frank, J. D. (1961). *Persuasion and healing*. Baltimore, MD: Johns Hopkins University Press.

Ginsburg, B., & Vogelsong, E. (1977). Premarital relationship improvement by maximizing empathy and self-disclosure: The primes program. In G. B. Guerney (Ed.), *Relationship enhancement*. San Francisco: Jossey-Bass.

Glenn, N. D., & Weaver, C. N. (1977). The marital happiness of remarried divorced persons. *Journal of Marriage and the Family*, *39*, 331–337.

Glick, P. C. (1980). Remarriage: Some recent changes and variations. *Journal of Family Issues*, *1*, 455–478.

Glick, P. C. (1984). How American families are changing. *American Demographics*, *6*(1), 20–25.

Glick, P. C., & Norton, A. J. (1973). Perspectives on the recent upturn in divorce and remarriage. *Demography*, *10*, 301–314.

Goldsmith, J. B., & McFall, R. M. (1975). Development and evaluation of an interpersonal skill-training program for psychiatric inpatients. *Journal of Abnormal Psychology*, *84*, 51–58.

Goldstein, A. (1962). *Therapist-patient relationships in psychotherapy*. New York: Macmillan.

Gottman, J. M. (1979). *Marital interaction: Experimental investigations*. New York: Academic Press.

Gottman, J. M., Markman, H., & Notarius, C. (1977). The topography of marital conflict: A sequential analysis of verbal and nonverbal behavior. *Journal of Marriage and the Family*, *39*, 461–477.

Gottman, J. M., Notarius, C., Gonso, J., & Markman, H. (1976). *A couple's guide to communication*. Champaign, IL: Research Press.

Gottman, J. M., Notarius, C., Markman, H., Bank, S., Yoppi, B., & Rubin, M. E. (1976). Behavior exchange theory and marital decision making. *Journal of Personality and Social Psychology*, *34*, 14–23.

Gottman, J. M., & Porterfield, A. L. (1981). Communicative competence in nonverbal behavior of married couples. *Journal of Marriage and the Family*, *43*, 817–824.

Greer, R. D., & Polirstok, S. R. (1982). Collateral gains and short term maintenance in reading and on-task responses by inner-city adolescents as a function of their use of social reinforcement while tutoring. *Journal of Applied Behavior Analysis*, *15*, 123–139.

Gurman, A. S., & Kniskern, D. P. (1978). Research on marital and family therapy: Progress, perspective, and prospect. In S. L. Garfield & A. E. Bergin (Eds.), *Handbook of psychotherapy and behavior change: An empirical analysis* (pp. 817–901). New York: Wiley.

Gurman, A. S., & Kniskern, D. P. (1981). *Handbook of family therapy*. New York: Brunner/Mazel.

Hatfield, E., & Walster, G. W. (1978). *A new look at love*. Reading, MA: Addison-Wesley.

Heller, K., & Monahan, J. (1977). *Psychology and community change.* Homewood, IL: Dorsey Press.

Henderson, J. (1975). Object relations and a new social psychiatry: The illusion of primary prevention. *Bulletin of the Menninger Clinic, 39,* 233–245.

Hetherington, E. M. (1979). Divorce: A child's perspective. *American Psychologist, 34,* 851–858.

Hops, H., Wills, T. A., Patterson, G. R., & Weiss, R. L. (1972). *Marital interaction coping system.* Eugene, OR: University of Oregon and Oregon Research Institute.

Isbister, J. (1975). Speech before the Southern Branch, American Public Health Association, Houston, Texas.

Jacobson, N. S. (1977). Problem solving and contingency contracting in the treatment of marital discord. *Journal of Consulting and Clinical Psychology, 45,* 92–100.

Jacobson, N. S. (1978). A review of the research on the effectiveness of marital therapy. In T. J. Paolino & B. S. McCrady (Eds.), *Marriage and marital therapy: Psychoanalytic, behavioral and systems theory perspectives* (pp. 395–444). New York: Brunner/Mazel.

Jacobson, N. S. (1979). Increasing positive behaviors in severely distressed adult relationships: The effectiveness of problem-solving training. *Behavior Therapy, 10,* 311–326.

Jacobson, N. S. (1981). Behavioral marital therapy. In A. S. Gurman & D. P. Kniskern (Eds.), *Handbook of family therapy* (pp. 556–591). New York: Brunner/Mazel.

Jacobson, N. S., & Bussod, N. (1983). Marital and family therapy. In M. Hersen, A. E. Kazdin, & A. S. Bellack (Eds.), *The clinical psychology handbook* (pp. 611–630). Elmsford, NY: Pergamon.

Jacobson, N. S., Elwood, R. W., & Dallas, M. (1981). Assessment of marital dysfunction. In D. H. Barlow (Ed.), *Behavioral assessment of adult disorders* (pp. 439–479). New York: Guilford Press.

Jacobson, N. S., & Margolin, G. (1979). *Marital therapy: Strategies based on social learning and behavior exchange principles.* New York: Brunner/Mazel.

Jacobson, N. S., & Martin, B. (1976). Behavioral marriage therapy: Current status. *Psychological Bulletin, 83,* 540–556.

Jacobson, N. S., McDonald, D. W., Follette, W. C., & Berley, R. A. (in press). Attributional processes in distressed and nondistressed married couples. *Cognitive Therapy and Research.*

Jacobson, N. S., Waldron, H., & Moore, D. (1980). Toward a behavioral profile of marital distress. *Journal of Consulting and Clinical Psychology, 48,* 696–703.

Johnston, J. M., & Johnston, G. T. (1972). Modification of consonant speech-sound articulation in young children. *Journal of Applied Behavior Analysis, 5,* 233–246.

Jourard, S. M. (1968). *Disclosing man to himself.* New York: Van Nostrand Reinhold.

Jourard, S. M. (1971). *The transparent self.* New York: Van Nostrand Reinhold.

Kahn, M. (1970). Nonverbal communication and marital satisfaction. *Family Process, 9,* 449–456.

Kaslow, F. W. (1981). Divorce and divorce therapy. In A. S. Gurman & D. P. Kniskern (Eds.), *Handbook of family therapy* (pp. 662–696). New York: Brunner/Mazel.

Kelley, H. H. (1973). The process of causal attribution. *American Psychologist, 28,* 107–128.

Kessler, M., & Albee, G. W. (1977). An overview of the literature on primary prevention. In G. W. Albee & J. M. Jaffe (Eds.), *Primary prevention of psychopathology, Vol. I: The issues.* Hanover, NH: University Press of New England.

Klein, D. C., & Goldston, S. E. (1977). *Primary prevention: An idea whose time has come.* Washington, DC: U.S. Government Printing Office.

Klier, J. L., & Rothberg, M. (1977). *Characteristics of conflict resolution in couples.* Paper presented at the 11th Annual Convention of the Association for the Advancement of Behavior Therapy, Atlanta, GA.

Knox, D. (1985). *Choices in relationships: An introduction to marriage and the family.* St. Paul, MN: West Publishing Co.

Kurdek, L. A. (1981). An integrative perspective of children's divorce adjustment. *American Psychologist, 36*, 856–866.

Kurland, M. (1953). Romantic love and economic considerations: A cultural comparison. *Journal of Educational Sociology, 27* (October), 72–79.

Larsen, D., Attkisson, C., Hargreaves, W., & Nguyen, T. (1979). Assessment of client/patient satisfaction: Development of a general scale. *Evaluation and Program Planning, 2*, 197–207.

Larzelere, R. E., & Huston, T. L. (1980). The dyadic trust scale: Toward understanding interpersonal trust in close relationships. *Journal of Marriage and the Family, 42*, 595–604.

Lederer, W. J., & Jackson, D. D. (1968). *Mirages of marriage*. New York: Norton.

Levinger, G., & Senn, D. J. (1967). Disclosure of feelings in marriage. *Merrill-Palmer Quarterly of Behavior and Development, 13*, 237–249.

Linehan, K. S., & Rosenthal, T. L. (1979). Current behavioral approaches to marital and family therapy. *Advances in Behaviour Research and Therapy, 2*, 99–143.

Locke, H. J., Sabagh, G., & Thomas, M. M. (1956). Correlates of primary communication and empathy. *Research Studies of the State College of Washington, 24*, 116–124.

Locke, H. J., & Wallace, K. M. (1959). Short-term marital adjustment and prediction tests: Their reliability and validity. *Journal of Marriage and Family Living, 21*, 251–255.

Mace, D. R. (1972). *Getting ready for marriage*. Nashville, TN: Abingdon.

Margolin, G. (1981). Practical applications of behavioral marital assessment. In E. E. Filsinger & R. A. Lewis (Eds.), *Assessing marriage: New behavioral approaches* (pp. 90–109). Beverly Hills, CA: Sage.

Margolin, G., & Jacobson, N. S. (1981). Assessment of marital dysfunction. In M. Hersen & A. S. Bellack (Eds.), *Behavioral assessment: A practical handbook* (pp. 389–426). Elmsford, NY: Pergamon.

Margolin, G., & Weiss, R. L. (1978). Comparative evaluation of therapeutic components associated with behavioral marital treatment. *Journal of Consulting and Clinical Psychology, 46*, 1476–1486.

Marital Studies Center (1975). *Marital interaction coding system (MICS): Training and reference manual for coders*. Unpublished manuscript, University of Oregon, Eugene, OR.

Markman, H. J. (1979). Application of a behavioral model of marriage in predicting relationship satisfaction of couples planning marriage. *Journal of Consulting and Clinical Psychology, 47*, 743–749.

Markman, H. J., & Floyd, F. (1980). Possibilities for the prevention of marital distress: A behavioral perspective. *American Journal of Family Therapy, 8*, 29–48.

Markman, H. J., Floyd, F., & Dickson-Markman, F. (1984). Toward a model for the prediction and primary prevention of marital and family distress and dissolution. In S. Duck (Ed.), *Personal relationships 4: Dissolving personal relationships*. London: Academic Press.

Markman, H. J., Notarius, C. I., Stephen, C. I., & Smith, R. J. (1981). Behavioral observation systems for couples: The current status. In E. E. Filsinger & R. A. Lewis (Eds.), *Assessing marriage: New behavioral approaches* (pp. 234–262). Beverly Hills, CA: Sage.

McFall, R. M. (1982). A review and reformulation of the concept of social skills. *Behavioral Assessment, 4*, 1–33.

McFall, R. M., & Dodge, K. A. (1982). Self-management and interpersonal skills learning. In P. Karoly & F. H. Kanfer (Eds.), *Self-management and behavior change: From theory to practice* (pp. 353–392). Elmsford, NY: Pergamon.

Meadow, M. E., & Taplin, J. F. (1970). Premarital counseling with college students: A promising triad. *Journal of Counseling Psychology, 17*, 516–518.

Mehrabian, A. (1972). *Nonverbal communication*. Chicago, IL: Aldine Atherton.

Miller, S., Nunnally, E., & Wackman, D. (1975). *Alive and aware*. Minneapolis, MN: Interpersonal Communications Program.

Murphy, K. C., & Strong, S. R. (1972). Some effects of similarity self-disclosure. *Journal of Counseling Psychology, 19,* 121–124.

National Center for Health Statistics (1984). Births, marriages, divorces, and deaths for 1983. *Monthly Vital Statistics Report,* 32: DHHS Pub. No. (PHS) 84-1120. Hyattsville, MD: U. S. Public Health Service.

Navran, L. (1967). Communication and adjustment in marriage. *Family Process, 6,* 173–184.

Nelson, R. O. (1981). Realistic dependent measures for clinical use. *Journal of Consulting and Clinical Psychology, 49,* 168–182.

Olson, D. (1978). Insiders' and outsiders' view of relationships: Research strategies. In G. Levinger & H. L. Raush (Eds.), *Close relationships.* Amherst, MA: University of Massachusetts Press.

Olson, D. H., & Ryder, R. G. (1970). Inventory of marital conflicts. *Journal of Marriage and the Family, 32,* 443–448.

Otto, H. A. (1976). *Marriage and family enrichment: New perspectives and programs.* Nashville, TN: Parthenon Press.

Palazzoli-Selvini, M., Boscolo, L., Cecchin, G., & Prata, G. (1978). A ritualized prescription in family therapy: Odd days and even days. *Journal of Marriage and Family Counseling, 4,* 3–9.

Patterson, G. R. (1976). Some procedures for assessing changes in marital interaction patterns. *Oregon Research Institute Bulletin,* Entire No. 16.

Patterson, G. R., & Reid, J. B. (1970). Reciprocity and coercion: Two facets of social systems. In C. Neuringer & J. Michael (Eds.), *Behavior modification in clinical psychology* (pp. 133–177). New York: Appleton-Century-Crofts.

Paul, G. L., & Lentz, R. J. (1977). *Psychosocial treatment of chronic mental patients: Milieu versus social-learning programs.* Cambridge, MA: Harvard University Press.

Phillips, E. L. (1978). *The social skills basis of psychopathology.* New York: Grune & Stratton.

Phillips, E. L., Phillips, E. A., Fixsen, D. L., & Wolf, M. M. (1971). Achievement phase: Modification of the behaviors of pre-delinquent boys within a token economy. *Journal of Applied Behavior Analysis, 4,* 45–49.

Prochaska, J., & Prochaska, J. (1978). Twentieth century trends in marriage and marital therapy. In T. J. Paolino & B. S. McCrady (Eds.), *Marriage and marital therapy: Psychoanalytic, behavioral, and systems theory perspectives* (pp. 1–24). New York: Brunner/Mazel.

Raush, H. L., Barry, W. A., Hertel, R. K., & Swain, M. A. (1974). *Communication, conflict, and marriage.* San Francisco: Jossey-Bass.

Resick, P. A., Sweet, J. J., Kieffer, D. M., Barr, P. K., & Ruby, N. L. (1977). *Perceived and actual discriminations of conflict and accord in marital communication.* Paper presented at the 11th Annual Convention of the Association for the Advancement of Behavior Therapy, Atlanta, GA.

Resick, P. A., Welsh-Osga, B., Zitomer, E. A., Spiegel, D. K., Meidlinger, J. C., & Long, B. R. (1980). *Predictors of marital satisfaction, conflict, and accord: Study 1, a preliminary revision of the marital interaction coding system.* Unpublished manuscript, University of South Dakota, Vermillion, SD.

Rettig, K. D., & Bulboz, M. M. (1983). Interpersonal resource exchanges as indicators of quality of marriage. *Journal of Marriage and the Family, 45,* 497–509.

Riskin, J., & Faunce, C. E. (1972). An evaluative review of family interaction research. *Family Process, 11,* 365–455.

Rutledge, A. L. (1966). *Premarital counseling.* Cambridge, MA: Schenkman Press.

Sager, C. J. (1976). *Marriage contracts and couple therapy: Hidden forces in intimate relationships.* New York: Brunner/Mazel.

Schlein, S. (1971). *Training dating couples in empathic and open communication: An experimental evaluation of a potential preventive mental health program*. Unpublished doctoral dissertation, Pennsylvania State University, University Park, PA.

Snyder, D. K. (1979a). *Marital Satisfaction Inventory*. Los Angeles: Western Psychological Services.

Snyder, D. K. (1979b). Multidimensional assessment of marital satisfaction. *Journal of Marriage and the Family, 41*, 813–823.

Snyder, D. K. (1981). *Manual for the Marital Satisfaction Inventory*. Los Angeles: Western Psychological Services.

Spanier, G. B. (1976). Measuring dyadic adjustment: New scales for assessing the quality of marriage and similar dyads. *Journal of Marriage and the Family, 38*, 15–28.

Stokes, T. F., & Baer, D. M. (1977). An implicit technology of generalization. *Journal of Applied Behavior Analysis, 10*, 349–367.

Stokes, T. F., Baer, D. M., & Jackson, R. L. (1974). Programming the generalization of a greeting response in four retarded children. *Journal of Applied Behavior Analysis, 7*, 599–610.

Strodtbeck, F. L. (1951). Husband–wife interaction over revealed differences. *American Sociological Review, 16*, 468–473.

Stuart, R. B. (1980). *Helping couples change*. New York: Guilford.

Stuart, R. B., & Lott, L. A. (1972). Behavioral contracting with delinquents: A cautionary note. *Journal of Behavior Therapy and Experimental Psychiatry, 3*, 161–169.

Tennov, D. (1979). *Love and limerance*. New York: Stein & Day.

Thibaut, J. W., & Kelley, H. H. (1959). *The social psychology of groups*. New York: Wiley.

Thomas, E. J. (1977). *Marital communication and decision-making*. New York: The Free Press.

Thomas, E. J., Walter, C. L., & O'Flaherty, K. A. (1974). A verbal problem checklist for use in assessing family verbal behavior. *Behavior Therapy, 5*, 235–246.

Turkewitz, H., O'Leary, K. D., & Ironsmith, M. (1975). Generalization and maintenance of appropriate behavior through self-control. *Journal of Consulting and Clinical Psychology, 43*, 559–583.

Villard, K., & Whipple, L. (1976). *Beginnings in relational communication*. New York: Wiley.

Vincent, J. P., Friedman, L. L., Nugent, J., & Messerly, L. (1979). Demand characteristics in observations of marital interaction. *Journal of Consulting and Clinical Psychology, 47*, 557–566.

Vincent, J. P., Weiss, R. L., & Birchler, G. R. (1975). A behavioral analysis of problem-solving in distressed and nondistressed married and stranger dyads. *Behavior Therapy, 6*, 475–487.

Watzlawick, P., Beavin, J. H., & Jackson, D. D. (1967). *Pragmatics of human communication*. New York: Norton.

Weathers, L., & Liberman, R. (1975). Contingency contracting with families of delinquent adolescents. *Behavior Therapy, 6*, 356–366.

Weeks, G., & L'Abate, L. (1982). *Paradoxical therapy: Theory and practice with individuals, couples, and families*. New York: Brunner/Mazel.

Weingarten, H. (1980). Remarriage and well-being. *Journal of Family Issues, 1*, 533–559.

Weiss, R. L. (1978). The conceptualization of marriage from a behavioral perspective. In T. J. Paolino & B. S. McCrady (Eds.), *Marriage and marital therapy: Psychoanalytic, behavioral and systems theory perspectives* (pp. 165–239). New York: Brunner/Mazel.

Weiss, R. L., & Birchler, G. R. (1978). Adults with marital dysfunction. In M. Hersen & A. S. Bellack (Eds.), *Behavior therapy in the psychiatric setting* (pp. 331–364). Baltimore, MD: Williams & Wilkins.

Weiss, R. L., Hops, H., & Patterson, G. R. (1973). A framework for conceptualizing marital conflict, a technology for altering it, some data for evaluating it. In L. A. Hamerlynck, L. C. Handy, & E. J. Mash (Eds.), *Behavior change: Methodology, concepts, and practice* (pp. 309–342). Champaign, IL: Research Press.

Weiss, R. L., & Margolin, G. (1977). Assessment of marital conflict and accord. In A. R.

Ciminero, K. S. Calhoun, & H. E. Adams (Eds.), *Handbook of behavioral assessment* (pp. 555–602). New York: Wiley.

Welsh-Osga, B., Resick, P. A., & Zitomer, E. A. (1981). *Revising the marital interaction coding system: Study II, Extension and cross-validation.* Unpublished manuscript, University of South Dakota, Vermillion, SD.

Wieder, G. B., & Weiss, R. L. (1980). Generalizability theory and the coding of marital interactions. *Journal of Consulting and Clinical Psychology, 48,* 469–477.

Wile, D. B. (1981). *Couples therapy: A nontraditional approach.* New York: Wiley-Interscience.

Williams, A. M. (1979). The quantity and quality of marital interaction related to marital satisfaction: A behavioral analysis. *Journal of Applied Behavior Analysis, 12,* 665–678.

Wills, T. A., Weiss, R. L., & Patterson, G. R. (1974). A behavioral analysis of the determinants of marital satisfaction. *Journal of Consulting and Clinical Psychology, 42,* 802–811.

Wills, X. X., & Snyder, X. X. (1982). Clinical use of the marital satisfaction inventory: Two case studies. *The American Journal of Family Therapy, 10,* 17–26.

Wilson, G. L., & Bornstein, P. H. (1984). Paradoxical procedures and single-case methodology: Review and recommendations. *Journal of Behavior Therapy and Experimental Psychiatry, 15,* 195–203.

Yeaton, W. H., & Sechest, L. (1981). Critical dimensions in the choice and maintenance of successful treatments: Strength, integrity, and effectiveness. *Journal of Consulting and Clinical Psychology, 49,* 156–167.

Yelsma, P. (1984). Marital communication, adjustment and perceptual differences between "happy" and "counseling" couples. *The American Journal of Family Therapy, 12,* 26–36.

# Author Index

# Subject Index

# About the Authors

**Philip H. Bornstein** (PhD, The University of South Dakota) is a Professor of Psychology at The University of Montana. Dr. Bornstein's primary responsibilities are in the university's APA-approved graduate training program in clinical psychology. At the graduate level, his major courses of instruction include Marital/Family Therapy, Child Behavior Therapy, Seminars in Clinical Research, and Clinical Practicum. Dr. Bornstein also annually offers a large undergraduate class entitled the Psychology of Loving Relations. His latest publications have appeared in the *Journal of Marital and Family Therapy, American Journal of Family Therapy, Child and Family Behavior Therapy, Journal of Applied Behavior Analysis*, and *Journal of Behavior Therapy and Experimental Psychiatry*. Most recently, Dr. Bornstein has co-edited (with Alan Kazdin) the *Handbook of Clinical Behavior Therapy With Children* and presently serves on the editorial board of four major professional journals. In addition to the above, Dr. Bornstein is a member of local, state, and national boards; provides workshops, training seminars, and institutes; and maintains an active private practice in clinical psychology.

**Marcy Tepper Bornstein** (MA, The University of Montana) is presently a graduate student in the APA-approved clinical psychology training program at The University of Montana. Her major areas of interest currently include treatment programs for children of divorce, eating-related disorders (anorexia and bulimia), and techniques of marital/family therapy. Ms. Bornstein's most recent publications have appeared in *Behavior Therapy, American Journal of Family Therapy*, and the *Journal of Sex and Marital Therapy*. In addition, she has co-contributed chapters to the *Handbook of Behavioral Assessment* (Ciminero, Calhoun, & Adams) and *Child Behavioral Assessment: Principles and Procedures* (Ollendick & Hersen). Ms. Bornstein presently teaches coursework in The Psychology of Parent-Child Relations and has accepted an assistantship position at the University of Montana Center for Student Development for the 1985–86 academic year.

# Psychology Practitioner Guidebooks

Editors:
Arnold P. Goldstein, Syracuse University
Leonard Krasner, SUNY at Stony Brook
Sol L. Garfield, Washington University

Robert E. Becker, Richard G. Heimberg & Alan S. Bellack – *SOCIAL SKILLS TREATMENT FOR DEPRESSION*

Edward B. Blanchard & Frank Andrasik – *MANAGEMENT OF CHRONIC HEADACHES: A Psychological Approach*

Edward B. Blanchard, John E. Martin & Patricia M. Dubbert – *NON-DRUG TREATMENTS FOR ESSENTIAL HYPERTENSION*

Philip H. Bornstein & Marcy T. Bornstein – *MARITAL THERAPY: A Behavioral-Communications Approach*

Karen S. Calhoun & Beverly M. Atkeson – *TREATMENT OF VICTIMS OF SEXUAL ASSAULT*

Richard F. Dangel & Richard A. Polster – *TEACHING CHILD MANAGEMENT SKILLS*

Eva L. Feindler & Randolph B. Ecton – *ADOLESCENT ANGER CONTROL: Cognitive-Behavioral Techniques*

Paul Karoly & Mark P. Jensen – *MULTIMETHOD ASSESSMENT OF CHRONIC PAIN*

Edward A. Kirby & Liam K. Grimley – *UNDERSTANDING AND TREATING ATTENTION DEFICIT DISORDER*

Daniel S. Kirschenbaum, William G. Johnson & Peter M. Stalonas, Jr. – *TREATING CHILDHOOD AND ADOLESCENT OBESITY*

Donald Meichenbaum – *STRESS INOCULATION TRAINING*

Michael T. Nietzel & Ronald C. Dillehay – *PSYCHOLOGICAL CONSULTATION IN THE COURTROOM*

Elsie M. Pinkston & Nathan L. Linsk – *CARE OF THE ELDERLY: A Family Approach*

Alice W. Pope, Susan M. McHale & W. Edward Craighead – *SELF-ESTEEM ENHANCEMENT WITH CHILDREN AND ADOLESCENTS*

Walter B. Pryzwansky & Robert N. Wendt – *PSYCHOLOGY AS A PROFESSION: Foundations of Practice*

Michael C. Roberts – *PEDIATRIC PSYCHOLOGY*

Raymond G. Romanczyk – *CLINICAL UTILIZATION OF MICROCOMPUTER TECHNOLOGY*

Sebastiano Santostefano – *COGNITIVE CONTROL THERAPY WITH CHILDREN AND ADOLESCENTS*

C. Eugene Walker, Barbara L. Bonner & Keith L. Kaufman – *THE PHYSICALLY AND SEXUALLY ABUSED CHILD: Evaluation and Treatment*

Lillie Weiss, Melanie Katzman & Sharlene Wolchik – *TREATING BULIMIA: A Psychoeducational Approach*

Elizabeth Yost, Larry E. Beutler, Anne Corbishley & James Allender – *GROUP COGNITIVE THERAPY: A Treatment Method for the Depressed Elderly*